AMSTERDAM EXPOSED

AN AMERICAN'S JOURNEY INTO THE RED LIGHT DISTRICT

BY DAVID WIENIR

dW

DE WALLEN PRESS

dW

De Wallen Press
West Hollywood, California
dewallenpress@gmail.com

LIBRARY OF CONGRESS CATALOGING-IN-
PUBLICATION DATA
Wienir, David, author
Amsterdam exposed: an american's journey into the red light district /
David Wienir

Trade Paperback ISBN-13: 978-0-9993559-0-9
eBook ISBN-13: 978-0-9993559-1-6

1. Travel/Europe/Netherlands/Amsterdam 2. Biographies & Memoirs/
Travelers and Explorers
3. Romance/Multicultural

Printed in the United States of America

9 8 7 6 5 4 3 2

To my wife

Prologue

IT HAS BEEN said that nothing is permanent except for change itself. This holds true for both people and places, so it's not surprising that much has changed in Amsterdam since the events of this book took place. Much of that change, however, could never have been anticipated.

In recent years, efforts have been made to remove the red light district from the heart of the city, all in an attempt to reclaim and revitalize it. Entire rows of windows, where women have stood for centuries, are being shut. Historic streets are being redistricted. Essentially, working girls are being exiled from the city's core, and *coffeeshops* selling cannabis, which have attracted millions of tourists for years, have been closed as well. As much of the Western world has developed a growing acceptance of marijuana, especially for medicinal purposes, Holland has moved in the opposite direction. Legislation has even been proposed to treat cannabis with more than 15 percent THC as a hard drug, and make coffeeshops available only to the Dutch. As a result, the red light district that has persevered and flourished for hundreds of years in Amsterdam may soon be finished.

The story told in this book will take you on an intimate and unprecedented journey into that world, perhaps for the last time. This is not a work of fiction masquerading as fact. Only names have been changed. The book tells the true story of an innocent exchange student who moves to Holland hoping to write a book about the red light district and everything that follows. It's a story of exploration. It's a story of friendship. It's a story of the search for innocence in a place bereft thereof. It's a story of change, and it's a story that will hopefully not only touch you, but forever reshape your understanding of the red light district and the women who work there.

I began working on this book in 1999 as the events happened, just days before the turn of the millennium. It has taken me almost two decades to share it with the world. There were times I thought the book would never be published. My life had evolved, and when lives do, stories go untold. My career had taken me into corporate America, with stints at several prestigious law firms. I represented clients such as Steven Spielberg and Madonna, and knew many lawyers would be quick to judge a book of this nature, given the subject matter and everything that comes along with it. I would be judged, too. There is nothing corporate America likes less than someone trying to change the status quo, or worse, someone who strays from the herd. With rent to pay and a fragile career in the making, I was not yet ready to rock the boat.

Over the years, I worked intermittently on the manuscript. Some years I did very little. In others, I did more. In every year, my perspective on the story changed. Ultimately, something kept me coming back. I struggled to figure out what it was. It wasn't just a story of a 26-year-old American in Europe. It wasn't just a story of someone trying to do the impossible, and it wasn't just a promise that had to be kept. It's simply a story that must be told. There's never been another one like it.

A final note before we begin: for those politically correct readers, or those easily offended, it is my sincere hope that you will love this book, but be forewarned it is very real. I didn't soften the edges—at all. To do so would be inauthentic, and defeat the purpose. I saw what I saw. What happened, happened. So hold on tight as we dive in deep, and apologies to anyone rubbed the wrong way. That was not my intention. Lastly, if you are under 18 and reading this, best to put it down until you come of age. Otherwise, reader beware. With that, let the journey begin.

Chapter 1

"AMSTERDAM IS IN my heart," she said as she clutched the purple nylon shirt that clung tightly to her chest. "Amsterdam, it is life."

Inga had only lived in Holland for two months and had already been bewitched by the infamous Dutch town. As we walked down Haarlemmerstraat in the direction of the central station, I had not much to add to the conversation. Not yet. I had only been in Amsterdam for a few hours. The city had yet to make its impression.

That said, this wasn't my first time in town, though it had been a while. Like so many Americans, I had backpacked through Amsterdam while an undergrad during a year abroad. I visited the Van Gogh Museum, the Anne Frank House, and a live sex show, all must-see attractions.

Back then my trip was an innocent one. At the time, I had never even tried weed. I grew up on a cul-de-sac in the San Fernando Valley, went to an all-boys high school, and had very little contact with anything having to do with drugs. It was not a part of my upbringing, or something I was interested in. I even remember reprimanding one of my friends for smoking weed before going into the Van Gogh Museum. As for sex, well, I grew up in the height of the AIDS epidemic. We were taught to associate sex with death. It was terrifying, and I got off to a late start. When walking through the red light district during that first trip, I walked fast. I tried to not make eye contact with anyone, and wanted to get out of there as soon as possible. I never imagined living in Amsterdam, or even returning. Six years after my first visit, the forces of my life were taking me back.

I was entering my third year of law school at Berkeley and about to begin a career in international law. The school agreed to give me a full semester of credit to study in Amsterdam. Many thought I was crazy for leaving Berkeley for even a semester. This was not the normal path. As Holland is an important center of international law, I tried but couldn't think of a good reason not to go.

Also, I definitely needed a break from Berkeley. My second book decrying the lack of intellectual diversity at the law school had just been published—during my second year. Essentially, the book was about the inherent worth of the individual, a theme that runs through this one as well. It created controversy and attracted national attention. The premise was simple. In the name of diversity, you shouldn't shout down people who disagree with you. Especially regarding controversial issues, and especially at a top law school. This was a lot for Berkeley to handle. After a tumultuous book release, I looked forward to some time away.

While most of my class remained in California for the summer, I took a job in New York at Coudert Brothers, the oldest international law firm in America. Back in the day, being a summer associate was like going to adult summer camp. Very little work was done or expected, and days were spent being wined and dined. There were about 30 of us in the program, mostly from top law schools. We were constantly told how great we were, despite having accomplished very little, if anything, in the real world. We would go on scavenger hunts, river cruises, country club retreats, and whatever else they could think of, all to get us to sell our souls after graduation. It was a scary time. After all, once you sell your soul, you can never get it back. You could feel it in the air, and see it in the faces around us. There was something soulless about the place.

What was most frightening was that, for many of us, our lives had taken us to this place without ever making a single career decision. We were told if we worked hard, we would have opportunities down the road. We believed them. We made sacrifices in high school to get into an elite college, and then even more to get into a top law school. We pursued all this with the understanding law school opens doors and creates opportunities. Suddenly, there we were, saddled with monstrous debt and being led into a life most of us would never escape, and many would deeply regret.

I called this the opportunity myth. It is real, devastating, and fueled by law schools that care more about their endowments than the well-being of their students. After three months of wearing Brooks Brothers suits, the other summer associates went back to their respective law schools. My decision to go to Amsterdam was about much more than international law, or getting away from Berkeley. It was about breaking free.

With the summer program over, on a brisk September morning, I put on a pair of blue jeans and a white T-shirt and boarded a plane to Amsterdam. I traveled light. If necessary, I could do some shopping in town.

Money was an issue, and the cheapest flight I could find was on Iceland Air. This allowed for a three-day layover in Reykjavik. I had always dreamed of visiting Iceland and decided to spend a few days there. With a copy of *Let's Go Europe* serving as my bible, I found a bed in the Salvation Army Guesthouse. Back then, there were two travel guides in play, *Let's Go Europe* and the *Lonely Planet*. *Let's Go Europe* was the guide of choice for students, effectively funneling everyone into the same hostels, restaurants, landmarks, and clubs. Within minutes, I connected with a group of international students. We spent the next three days touring waterfalls, enjoying the local cuisine, and bonding.

On our final day, we visited the waters of the Blue Lagoon. There were six of us, from six different countries. Submerged to our shoulders, we floated in silence, looking into each other's eyes and carving out the moment. After a night partying in Reykjavik, we said our goodbyes, knowing we would never see each other again. That was OK. This was just a layover. I continued on my journey refreshed, feeling as if I had visited the moon.

I arrived in Amsterdam's Schiphol Airport knowing three things, more or less. First, I knew I would be studying law at the Vrije Universiteit Amsterdam, one of the two major universities in town. Second, I knew the address of my apartment. Third, I knew I would be there for four months. Then, I would have to return to Berkeley for my final semester.

After clearing customs, I hopped on a train to Amsterdam's central station, making sure to steer clear of the gypsies and pickpockets who notoriously preyed on that stretch of rail. I had been warned to never stand by the doors, the prime spot where thieves would snatch and run, so I tightly wedged myself into a pack of tall Dutchmen. I arrived exhausted and blanketed with Dutch B.O., but without incident. I then hailed myself a cab. To get a good exchange rate, I bought a few hundred guilders back home. In 1999 the US economy was strong, with one dollar worth roughly two guilders. For an American stepping foot in Holland, everything was half price.

As I entered the cab, I reached into my pocket and pulled out a piece of paper with the address of my new home. It read Planciusstraat 13. I knew it was nearby, but that's all. I looked at the paper and did my best to pronounce the name. I'm not sure what came out of my mouth, but it was ugly, and it wasn't Dutch. The driver looked at me blankly, shaking his head. I gave it another try, changing it up a bit, and again, the same response. I had butchered it once more. After one more attempt, I surrendered and handed the crumpled piece of paper to the driver.

"Ah, Planciusstraat," he said with a smile and began driving west.

Within ten minutes, we arrived. The building was located about a mile northwest of the central station in a district called Westelijke Eilanden. This was one of the up-and-coming areas in the city, full of art galleries and lofts. While home to some of the most picturesque and traditional buildings in Amsterdam, boasting rows of painted shutters and geometric roofs, Planciusstraat 13 was humble. Basically, it was a nondescript, six-story, brick building just down the street from a herring stand.

Not yet realizing the Dutch rarely, if ever, tip, I gave the driver a few extra guilders. He accepted the money with a look of surprise and helped me to the door. After getting the keys from the landlord and signing a two-page lease, which thankfully had been translated into English, I was directed to a room on the third floor. Rent was cheap at 600 guilders a month, roughly $300.

The room was small and barely fit a bed, mini fridge, and sink. A balcony looked out onto a canal. It was the classic Amsterdam view, like something you might see on a postcard. I gazed out the window as a boat floated by. It was packed with tourists sipping wine, eating cheese squares, and taking pictures of the historic buildings huddled around my apartment. I waved as they passed. Someone snapped a picture. I felt connected. Amsterdam felt right. The apartment was perfect. Well, except for one thing. Every few minutes, the No. 3 tram roared down the street, rattling the building. The sound was intense, like an earthquake.

By the time I unpacked my belongings, the room looked about as barren as when I arrived. Exhausted from the long day of travel, I stretched out on my bed like a starfish and wondered about the life I would soon create for myself.

Just as I closed my eyes, I was awoken by the sounds of a French horn from across the hall. It was loud, and the musician was a beginner trying to play the theme song from *Rocky*. Over and over, the same song played, again and again. Every time, wrong. Combined with the sounds of the No. 3 tram, I was about to lose my mind. I stumbled across the hall and knocked on the door, hoping to make an introduction, possibly a friend, and most importantly, stop the music. I needed sleep.

The music stopped and the door swung open. In front of me stood a 21-year-old Dutchman, slightly bewildered, his hair a mess.

"Hi, I'm David," I began.

"Hi," he replied, and nothing more. I waited to see if he was going to continue, maybe say his name or something. He didn't. He just stood there, gazing at me like a deer in headlights.

"I just moved here from America," I continued. "Nice playing."

"Thanks," he said, embarrassed but flattered. "You could hear?"

"Uh, yeah," I said, laughing. "I think all Amsterdam could."

"Oh, man, sorry," he said, dropping his head. "My name's Oliver. Want to come in?"

"Sure," I said, making my way through a pile of school-books, pizza boxes, and dirty socks to the only chair in the room. Oliver sat on the corner of his bed as *The A-Team* played in the background. The show was popular in Holland at the time, albeit 16 years after its American release.

"See," Oliver said, "it's in English."

Unlike most of Europe, American television isn't dubbed in the Netherlands. It's subtitled. The English voice remains. People wonder why the Dutch speak English so well compared to the French, Spanish, and so many others. It's simple. They were raised watching *The A-Team* and other quality US programming. In many respects, the Netherlands is bilingual because of it.

Consequently, the need for me to learn Dutch was more of a novelty than necessity. Nevertheless, when in a foreign country, it's always good to pick up a thing or two. It's a show of respect, and can open doors. I've always made it a rule to do so, and learned the basics upon my arrival. My first words were *doei, dank u wel, alstublieft,* and *je bent zo mooi.* Meaning "goodbye," "thank you," "please," and, "you're so beautiful." The essentials.

After a few minutes of *The A-Team* and some small talk, Oliver asked, "What brings you to Amsterdam?"

"I'm studying law at the Vrije Universiteit."

"Where?" Oliver asked.

"The Vrije Universiteit," I repeated, doing my best with the pronunciation.

"Huh?" Oliver said, lost.

"The Free University," I said, switching to English.

"Ah, the VU," he said enthusiastically, pronouncing it like "vew." "I'm at UVA, the other university in town."

"Cool," I replied, thrilled we got past that. "But really," I continued, "I'm here to write a book."

From the beginning, I came to Amsterdam hoping to write a book about the red light district. Without question, the district is one of the most popular tourist attractions in Europe, with over two and a half million visitors a year. Most explore Amsterdam for only a few days and leave with questions and misconceptions, like I had in the past. Many are haunted by what they see. I wanted to write a book that would not only answer those questions and dispel those misconceptions, but take readers on a journey deeper into the district than they could ever go before.

Moreover, most who visit the district form opinions about the women without speaking with them. That is their only option, unless they become a customer. Even then, the women keep to themselves. Dutch prostitutes have little interest talking to tourists. They have no interest befriending them. I wanted to introduce readers to women who had worked in the windows for years. I wanted readers to hear about the industry from their perspective. Nothing political, nothing contrived, and from a Dutch point of view.

I became interested in the topic of prostitution after finishing my first semester at Berkeley Law. It was an intense four months of civil procedure, torts, and criminal law. After surviving exams, a group of us decided to unwind by going to Reno, the biggest little city in the world. We shaved off our exam beards, grabbed a slice of pizza at Blondie's, Berkeley's famous pizza joint, and headed east. There were five of us, and it should have been a three-hour drive. Due to a snowstorm, the trip took seven hours. As we drove through the whiteout, we passed the time singing to '80s tunes and complaining about the lack of eligible women in law school.

Not surprisingly, Berkeley attracted a bit of an angry crowd, and dating was bleak. There is a saying that largely holds true: while New Yorkers define themselves by how much money they make, and people in LA define themselves by how they look and whom they know, people in the Bay Area define themselves by how angry they are. The way they see it, if you aren't angry, you don't care. Literally minutes after finishing exams, we were out of there.

It was a slow and twisting drive to Reno, but by nine o'clock we had checked into the Silver Legacy Casino and had been gambling for an hour. Inspired by the movie *Swingers*, we looked sharp. For the night, we were no longer students. We were dressed to impress. I spent most of my time playing craps and drinking triple gin and tonics. My strategy was solid—play the pass line, place six and eight, and avoid everything else, particularly the Iron Cross. It was all about discipline, and sticking to the plan. By 10 o'clock, I was up $500. The table was rocking. I had a roll that lasted 10 minutes. I was on fire. Feeling lucky, I kept going, betting hard ways and playing the field. I couldn't lose.

By 11 o'clock, I was down $400. Defeated, I retreated from the table and hit the nickel slots with a group of chain-smoking grandmas from Germany. They took a liking to me, mostly due to my suit. I had taken Reno by storm.

We topped off the night at an all-you-can-eat buffet and then a nightclub. By three o'clock, we were ready to call it quits. Exhausted, we went outside in the cold and waited for a cab. After 20 minutes, one arrived.

The driver was a thin man in his fifties with a thick mustache and sun-damaged skin. He wore a plaid suit and seemed to take pride in his job. He got out of the cab and opened the back door. A sea of cigar smoke spilled out as he ushered us in. The car reeked, but we weren't about to wait for another. I sat in front. My friends climbed in back. Once on our way, the driver asked if we wanted to stop off for a snack at the ranch.

"Nah," I said, with the others agreeing. "Just take us to the Silver Legacy, please."

The driver continued, "They have a nice bar. You should check it out."

Other than hanging with the grandmas, the night had been a bust. This was our last chance to make something happen. I looked back at my friends who seemed open to the idea. It had been hours since the buffet, and a late-night snack sounded good. With a nod of my head, the driver began the short drive into the Nevada desert.

"You guys in school?" he asked, keeping the conversation moving.

"Yeah," I quietly replied. "Law school."

"Lawyers, huh?" he said intensely. "Maybe I should do the world a favor and let you out right here." I looked at my friends, worried we were driving into the desert with a sociopath.

After a few seconds, he continued, "Ah, I'm just joking. But, speaking of jokes, here's one. What's the difference between a lawyer and a prostitute?" We all sat in silence.

"Ah, come on. You know this. The prostitute stops screwing you when you're dead! Here, how about this one. You have to know this one. What's the difference between a lawyer and a bucket of shit?" Again, we sat in silence, wondering what we had gotten ourselves into. "The bucket! The bucket's the difference!" he said, chuckling. "That one's my favorite, but don't mind me. You seem all right. You're just kids. Anyhow, I never judge people by what they do, even lawyers. After all, if there's anything I've learned, it's this—people end up in life where they think they belong."

He paused, only to continue, "Life is shaped by biology, circumstance, culture, and lots of other factors. But the fact remains, when it comes down to it, on a subconscious level, we put ourselves in life where we think we belong. Consciously, we might want to end up somewhere else, but that doesn't really matter, does it?"

The driver continued explaining his theory as we drove deeper into the darkness, sprinkling us with lawyer jokes along the way. Before long, the car stopped and he announced we had arrived at our destination. It was not what we were expecting. Not at all. In front of us was the Mustang Ranch, one of the most famous brothels in the world.

"You said you were taking us to a bar!" I proclaimed.

"This is a bar," he said, "and a brothel, too. It's legal here. Don't worry. Check it out. It'll be an educational experience."

Having driven all the way there, it seemed a shame to turn around and go home. My friends agreed. We asked the driver to wait outside, explaining we would only be a few minutes. We would just grab a drink. He agreed and kept the meter running. It was four thirty in the morning, and we should have been more tired than our bodies were willing to admit. It was our first time in a brothel, and we were excited. But also terrified. We had never done anything like this before.

From the outside, the Mustang Ranch looked like a bunch of low-income trailers surrounded by a metal fence. It was hardly glamorous. One by one, we passed through the gate until we were standing on the porch. Bunched in a tight group, we rang the buzzer. One of my friends got nervous and farted. The door opened just as the smell cleared, and we made our way in.

To our surprise, the setting was festive and relaxed. Madonna's "Material Girl" played over the speakers. A circular bar in the middle of the room sold souvenir T-shirts, mugs, and lighters. A bunch of women sat on velvet couches to our left. Other than the bartender, no other men were in sight.

Before we could make our way to the bar, 10 women jumped to attention. They formed a line as if in a pageant. We gazed at them, speechless. For the most part they were attractive, and the variety was impressive. There was a big-breasted blonde, a curly-haired brunette, a biker chick, a schoolgirl, a corporate type, and even the girl next door. Just about any sexual fantasy could be fulfilled with the swipe of a credit card.

After standing frozen for what seemed like minutes, the women got bored and returned to their couches. They could tell none of us were prepared to pull the trigger. They were right. Up until that moment, none of us had ever even considered visiting a prostitute. Long story short, we were a bunch of socially awkward Ivy League kids way out of our element. Also, I was pretty sure my friend who farted was a virgin. We sat at the bar and ordered our obligatory beers. The unspoken plan was that we would have a few sips and be on our way. After all, the cab was waiting and the meter running. Things didn't go according to plan. They rarely do.

It all happened quickly. A girl caught me looking and made her way over.

"Hi," she said, smiling.

"Hey," I replied, trying to play it cool.

"Can I help you with something? Do you like what you see?"

"You're beautiful, but this isn't my thing," I said. "We just stopped by for a drink."

"That's too bad," she said with a pout. "You're cute. Let me show you around. My name's Sarah."

My first reaction was to say no, but I stopped myself. What the hell—a tour's a tour. It would be rude to refuse.

Sarah took my hand and led me down a dimly lit hallway. My friends didn't hear the conversation. They just saw the action unfold and watched as I followed her into the brothel. Their jaws dropped as I turned around to indicate I would be back soon, or so I hoped.

Sarah showed me the jacuzzi rooms and executive suites as we walked down the hallway. As we passed a few locked doors, she apologized she couldn't give the full tour. I listened for the sounds of sex. All was quiet.

We ended up in her room. It was filled with personal belongings and stuffed animals, including a love-worn brown bear. I no longer felt like I was in a brothel, but a bedroom. Pictures of friends and family hung on the walls, along with a high school diploma. Sarah stretched out on her bed and invited me to lie down beside her. Soon, the two of us were side by side.

"Now that you're here, want to play?" she asked. "Talking is so overrated."

Looking at her, the last thing I saw was a prostitute. What I saw was a beautiful girl. Moralize all you want, but the situation was simple. We were two consenting adults who wanted to be together, albeit for different reasons. Had we met in public, far from the ranch, she could have been my dream girl. Circumstances were different. I had never paid for sex. I wasn't ready to cross that line.

"Sarah, you're gorgeous, but I can't do this," I said.

"I know, I could tell," she said. "It's OK. I'm pretty much done for the night anyway. We can just talk."

"I'd love that," I said, making myself comfortable. "I'm sure you've been asked a thousand times, but how did you end up here? There must be better ways to make a living."

"Ah, the golden question," she said. "I always wanted to be a lawyer, just like you. I thought about becoming a veterinarian, too. I love animals. I started working here because I needed money. One day, I just made the decision. My rent was due, and I needed cash. I heard about the place, and that was that.

"At the time, I didn't think much of it. At first, it was glamorous. Being the new girl was fun. I got all the attention. That faded, and now I can never go back—to the real world, that is. People forget we're human," she explained. "People hate us, even despise us. That is, except the guys who want to fuck us."

With that, she rolled over. "Sure you don't want to play? I'm really good at my job, and no one will ever know," she said, leaning close.

"I'm sorry," I said hesitantly.

I had so many questions. Sarah surely had other ways to make a living, yet here she was. I remembered the speech the cab driver gave when he said, "People end up in life where they think they belong." Ultimately, deep down, did Sarah think she belonged in such a place? Moreover, I wondered why a woman in need of understanding was afforded mostly contempt. Once she made the decision to start, society told her she was a whore, and would always be. She was trapped. There would be no turning back.

"Sarah, there's a customer for you," a voice outside the door said. "Are you free?"

Sarah looked at me. Placing a hand on the back of my neck, she drew me closer than I had ever been to a prostitute.

"Well, am I?" she asked, as her hand slid underneath my collar, her nails scratching my back.

"I really should go," I replied.

I was hardly convincing but Sarah didn't put up a fight. With a look of disappointment, she escorted me down the hallway where I found my friends waiting.

"It was nice chatting. Thanks for listening," she whispered.

That morning, with the cab waiting outside, I watched the sun rise over the Nevada desert from the window of a brothel. I felt inspired. Inspired to do what, I had no idea. I would figure that out later.

Chapter 2

OLIVER ASPIRED TO be a writer and instantly attached himself to me. Half Indonesian and half Dutch, he was raised in The Hague by a celebrated Dutch novelist. Now living in Amsterdam for the first time, he was ready for adventure.

"So, what's your plan for writing the book?" he asked.

"Plan?" I said, with an uneasy smile. I didn't really have one. I was fine with that, based on lessons I had learned years before.

After my freshman year in college, while my friends were securing internships in the business sector, I enrolled in whitewater rafting school in Idaho. My love for rafting ran deep, but while growing up, I never considered becoming a guide. I was being groomed for a different kind of life. Being a guide wasn't an option, or at least wasn't presented as one. My perspective changed while on a river trip during my senior year of high school. I was surprised to learn one of my guides was premed at Yale. I was off to Columbia in the fall. My mind was blown.

"If I can do it, why can't you?" she said. "Your identity is yours to choose."

A light went on. I wasn't stuck on a path at all. Corporate America would have to wait.

Guide school began in June, and conditions were extreme. The Middle Fork of the Salmon was running high, making the journey treacherous and unpredictable. We were in the wilderness for 15 days, and it rained nonstop. It was brutal, and we had to be careful. We had no idea what to expect downstream. When possible, we would climb the banks of the river to give us perspective on the rapids ahead. We would study the currents, noting side eddies and obstacles, and plot a course. Often, though, we had no choice but to enter the rapids blind.

I came to believe navigating life is very much like navigating a river. Each of our lives has a unique current. At certain times, we have more than one. They are never easy to find. Once we find our current, the trick is staying in it. There are many proverbial rocks and eddies confronting us every day. Some cling to them, or become stuck in them, and life passes them by—often due to fear, laziness, and other human foibles. While there are dangers ahead, there is also unimaginable beauty. Sometimes you can get a glimpse of what's to come; often you can't. Needless to say, you can never swim against the current, or create a path that's not yours. Doing so is futile, and can lead to ruin.

Seeing life like a river made sense, and guided me through my time in Amsterdam. What was my plan? I just needed to find my current, and stay in it. Everything else would follow.

With *The A-Team* over, I said goodbye to Oliver and returned to my room. Before leaving, Oliver gave me a bottle of Amstel as a housewarming gift. Exhausted, I put the beer in my fridge and slid into a deep sleep. But it wasn't easy. Oliver's horn had stopped, but the sounds of the No. 3 tram remained. Even with a pillow over my head and toilet paper in my ears, the sound was penetrating.

It has been said that everyone has a superpower. They just need to discover it. If I could be said to have such a thing, it would be to fall asleep anywhere, on command. Call me Captain Bedtime, The Super Sleeper, Siesta-Man, or whatever. They would all apply. Put me on a bus to Marrakesh, and boom. Within minutes, I can be under. Stick me on a train to Moscow with dogs barking down the aisle—still, no problem. The power was real, and turned out to be a lifesaver. But, even for Captain Bedtime, falling asleep on Planciusstraat took time. The noise was that bad.

After a few hours, I awoke at 10 p.m. to the sounds of knocking on my door. My room was pitch dark. Disoriented, for the first few seconds I thought I was back in New York. Then I remembered. I was living in Europe. The feeling of waking up in a foreign country, only to realize you are living there, is like none other. It's like being in a dream, yet being awake at the same time.

When I came to my senses and realized I was in Amsterdam, not New York, I assumed Oliver had stopped by for a visit. Still rubbing my eyes and with toilet paper in my ears, I opened the door in a pair of boxer shorts. To my surprise, standing in front of me was a short-haired girl.

"Oliver said you just flew in," she said. "Want me to show you around? My name's Inga."

"Sure," I said. "I'm David."

"You should probably put on some pants though, and take the paper out of your ears," she said, laughing politely. "I'll just wait in the hall."

I closed the door, put on pants, removed the toilet paper, and followed Inga to the basement where the bikes were parked. I watched as she unlocked the chains around one of the shittiest bikes I had ever seen. It was a green three-speeder that looked like it survived World War II.

"No bike yet, huh?" she asked.

"Nope. Do I need one?" I replied.

Inga looked at me in amazement. "Uh, yeah," she said. "But we'll be OK for tonight." Not having a bike in Amsterdam is like being a bird with its wings clipped. Inga was patient. It was my first night.

As I walked down Haarlemmerstraat in the light rain, with Inga pedaling in circles, she kept repeating, "Amsterdam is in my heart. Amsterdam, it is life." Each time, it was as if she was saying the words for the first time. To Inga, Amsterdam was more than just a city. It was a state of mind—and important to her soul. Little did I know, it would soon become important to mine as well.

Born in Vilnius, Inga had a more optimistic take on life than one would expect from someone who grew up behind the Iron Curtain. As we made our way down the street, I asked about her childhood. She said it was like living in hell.

"Life in Lithuania was depressing," she said. "People lived like ghosts trapped in a black-and-white world. There was no color anywhere. That is, except for the occasional rainbow. Not even the government could fuck that up. Worst of all, no one dreamed. What's the point? Here in Amsterdam, your life is yours to make. You can dream, and choose your path. Back home, people had no options. You lived for the state, and only the state. There was no such thing as self."

Inga's words resonated deeply. I too had experienced the blight of collectivism when I lived and worked in Tallinn just years after the collapse of the Soviet Union. While Estonia had since regained its independence, the aftereffects lingered, and the devastation was evident on the faces of everyone I encountered. I saw Inga as nothing less than a survivor, and witnessing her strength to persevere was inspiring. It was an affirmation of life, and the enduring nature of the human spirit. She refused to surrender.

As we proceeded down the street, the sounds of bicycle bells rang through the air. Like Inga's, most of the bikes looked days away from being scrapped. I was amazed some of them were even operational. Hoping not to offend her, I asked why so many bikes looked like shit.

She laughed. "This is Amsterdam," she said. "If you have a nice bike, you won't have it for long. It'll get pinched, so no one cares. People take pride in having a crap bike. I do," she said, honking her horn, which let out a sad squeal. "Who would steal this?"

While most of the bikes were certainly shitty, people boasted impressive if not superhuman skills from behind their rusted handlebars. It was like watching a roaming circus. One bike passed with three people on it. A girl sat in the biker's lap, facing backward, while another rode sideways on the luggage rack, eating fries. A few moments later, another biker passed, pedaling hands-free and holding two bikes side by side, all six wheels perfectly aligned.

As I watched in wonder, I noticed the letters XXX on metal poles lining the street.

"Are we in the red light district yet?" I asked, pointing at the penis-shaped barricades.

"No, those are just sidewalk barriers," Inga replied. "The Dutch call them *Amsterdammertjes*. XXX is Amsterdam's logo. It stands for charity, resolution, and heroism, or something like that."

Bikes are hard to ride at a walking pace, and Inga did a masterful job weaving back and forth as we continued down the street. After passing several kebab shops, we stopped in front of the yellow sign of the Victoria Hotel. Across from us was the central station, one of the most lavishly decorated stations in all of Europe. The person who designed the Rijksmuseum, Amsterdam's premier art museum, also designed the station back in the nineteenth century. Train stations are places of considerable drama and history, especially in Europe. This one was no different. For well over a century, the station has been the gateway to Amsterdam, through which billions have traveled—locals, tourists, and prostitutes alike, all anonymously passing each other, heading to worlds apart. The station was cloaked in mystery, and also a sense of timelessness, magnified by the thousands of corroded bikes locked around it.

As we stood facing the station, sounds of bagpipes filled the air. Odd for Amsterdam, I thought, as we were far from Scotland. Then a midget stumbled by walking a monkey on a leash. From the moment you stepped out of the station, the city was upon you.

Despite being a major European city, Amsterdam is very much a town. Far less intimidating than London, Paris, or Berlin, it's possible to bike just about anywhere in 20 minutes. The city was designed in the seventeenth century around a set of concentric horseshoe canals, like ripples in a pond, called the Grachtengordel. The central station is perched in the middle.

That is not the only reason Amsterdam is a biker's paradise. The city is completely flat. In fact, Amsterdam is several feet below sea level, dykes and canals being the only thing keeping the city from sinking into the sea. The country's name, the Netherlands, refers to the low-lying terrain, *nether* meaning "low" in Dutch. Holland is not the name of the country at all, but refers to the provinces of North Holland and South Holland, Amsterdam being located in the North.

Throughout the city, narrow four-story buildings line the canals. In fact, it's said the narrowest house in the world, measuring one meter wide, is located there. Years ago, Amsterdam assessed property value, and corresponding taxes, based on a building's width. As a result, buildings in Amsterdam are tall and narrow—so narrow, most are equipped with rooftop pulleys. Walking through town, it's not uncommon to see a piano or sofa suspended in midair, making its way into a window above.

Pedaling around the city is like roaming through an art gallery, or perhaps a science museum. Despite its compact size, almost 7,000 buildings fall under the jurisdiction of the government because of their aesthetic, scientific, and cultural significance. I say all this because many simply associate Amsterdam with weed and sex. There is so much more. While famous for its red lights, Amsterdam may be the most beautiful city in Europe, and possibly the world. As we made our way through the city that first night, I was in awe.

There are over 1,500 bridges in Amsterdam. Inga and I stopped on one of them. Reflections from the green lights of The Grasshopper, a Dutch coffeeshop, spilled into a canal full of boats and swans. Looking out over the city, Inga drew my attention to the spire of the Oude Kerk, or "old church," protruding over a row of buildings. It was like being in a living, breathing Van Gogh painting.

Inga led me down a damp metal stairway onto a round platform just above the water. The smell of Indonesian food filled the air as Inga pulled out a joint and took a hit.

"What are you doing?" I asked, looking for cops.

"Smoking a joint," she said calmly.

"Yeah, I see that," I said. "I thought you could only smoke in private, or in a coffeeshop."

"We should be fine," she said, holding the joint out in front of me. "Have a smoke."

"I'm OK," I replied.

"Sure?" she asked.

The thing was, I didn't come to Amsterdam to smoke. In fact, I never even tried weed until I was 21, and had only smoked once or twice since. But, there I was, in Amsterdam, and in the moment.

I looked at Inga and whispered, "OK, I'll have some."

Inga gave me a warm smile and passed the joint. I scanned for cops, took a drag, and passed it back like a hot potato.

"Americans," she said, laughing.

That night, standing on the bridge was the closest I came to the old church. Inga took me no farther. Instead, we meandered home, leaving the mysteries of the district hidden for at least one more night.

Chapter 3

I AWOKE 16 hours later to the sounds of Oliver playing his horn across the hall. My jet lag, combined with a little Dutch weed, had knocked me out. I slept through the day, and was feeling refreshed for the first time since leaving New York. As classes didn't start for a week, all was good. I was in my adjustment period.

I brushed my teeth in the room sink, grabbed the bottle of Amstel from my fridge, and opened the door to my balcony. It had just enough room to fit a folding chair, and I sat with my legs hanging over the rail. The sun shimmered on the canal as I took a swig of beer, the taste of toothpaste still in my mouth. I was living abroad, and in heaven.

The smell of basil and Parmesan lured me into the communal kitchen where I found Inga entertaining Oliver and a few international students. She stood over a stove preparing a special recipe of spaghetti carbonara while everyone drank Slovakian wine and sipped Red Bull. Inga invited me to join. I sat down as she served up a heaping plate of pasta. Red Bull had yet to catch on in America, and I was unfamiliar with the stuff. Inga warned to only drink one at a time. It was rumored drinking more could cause your heart to stop, possibly explode. There was even talk it contained bull semen. Regardless, Amsterdam was fueled by the drink. I quickly took a liking to it, hoping the rumors were just that—rumors.

Over the next hour, we relaxed and discussed the hot topics of the day. Bill Clinton, the death penalty, and why Americans are so fat. Was it diet? Lack of exercise? Portion size? Genetics? Who knew, but my European friends were fixated on the subject. Relatively speaking, it was an innocent time.

Without a doubt, being an American in Europe in the late '90s was different from today. For the first time, the world seemed to be coming together. We just got the World Wide Web. Travel was cheap. There was a growing sense of community, as cultural differences seemed less important than commonalities. The energy and excitement from the collapse of the Soviet Union spilled out across Europe, and the world seemed without boundary.

Economically, the dollar was strong, the Internet bubble was expanding, and the euro had yet to be adopted. After the euro replaced the guilder in 2002, life changed. Fifty guilders became 50 euros, effectively doubling the cost of everything overnight, from a kebab to a train ticket. Basically, the name changed, but not the number. For many Dutch, routine indulgences like drinking coffee in a café were transformed into luxuries. For Americans, our economic advantage evaporated. Back in 1999, these hard times were still around the corner.

Politically, America was largely seen as a benevolent power. Clinton was loved despite ruining Monica's dress, September 11 was just a day, and we were welcomed almost everywhere. Americans didn't need to apologize for being American. True, we were loved for our dollars, but there was something else. There was a fondness for us, and our optimistic take on life. Our values of individualism and self-reliance were celebrated. The world is now a different place. Looking back, it's safe to say these differences played a large role in how the next few months of my life would unfold.

After helping clean the kitchen, Oliver and I decided to take a walk around town. I was eager to continue exploring. When I asked Inga if she wanted to come, she said she couldn't. At first, she wouldn't say why. After pressing her, she explained her visa expired and she had to leave the next day. She had to return to Lithuania. Inga was so sad about it she wasn't planning on telling anyone. She was just going to disappear. She had no idea when she might return, if ever.

I had already taken a liking to her and was saddened by the news. Other than Oliver, she was my only friend in town. Back in 1999, there was no such thing as social media. Facebook wasn't launched until 2004, and email wasn't widely used. When it came to keeping in touch, options were limited. Phone calls were expensive. Writing letters wasn't realistic. As a result, friendships, even close ones, would vanish, forever, at a moment's notice. I would never communicate with my friends from Iceland again. Soon Inga, too, would be nothing more than a memory.

The world has since changed, but this was how it was. Goodbyes were forever, and absolute. Given these realities, people would rarely even ask each other's last name. It didn't matter. Inga was just Inga. Oliver and I gave her a hug goodbye never expecting to see her again, and headed on our way.

Saying goodbye to friends, forever, is never easy, and parting with Inga reminded me of a conversation I had with a friend at Oxford. He was reading for his doctorate and had been around the university for years. We ate every meal together, rowed in the same crew, and spent nights drinking port and reflecting on the meaning of life.

When my time in England was up, I asked for his address and phone number. I didn't want our friendship to end. It was too important. I would write. I would find a way to keep in touch. He nonchalantly said no, and then asked if I believed in Einstein's theory of relativity.

"Uh, I guess," I said, confused.

"So you believe time travel is theoretically possible, even if there are physical limitations to achieving it?"

"I guess," I said.

"Well, if time travel is theoretically possible, every moment that has happened, is happening, and will happen, is happening all at once. Simultaneously. We are stuck in a linear path and can only live in the present. But every moment is happening, over and over, in perpetuity." I listened carefully as he continued. "Accordingly, there are never real goodbyes. While we can't access those moments, they are here, and they are real."

The lesson he taught me remained. Once someone comes into your life, they can never leave. The moments are always there, around you. Knowing this made parting with Inga a bit easier. I only later learned this theory doesn't quite hold up. While it's theoretically possible to travel forward in time, you can never go back.

After leaving Inga, Oliver and I journeyed down Haarlemmerstraat to Dam Square. This was the obvious place to start our evening. Along with the central station, Dam Square is one of the main crossroads of the city. It's also home to the Royal Palace. The square was established in the thirteenth century when a dam was constructed on the Amstel River to prevent the city from flooding, hence its name. During the '60s, it became a meeting place for hippies and other freethinking folk. Long after the hippies took off, the square remained a popular gathering spot. As we entered, we passed the National Monument, a huge phallic sculpture centrally located in front of the Hotel Krasnapolsky.

Before continuing on our stroll, we decided to grab coffee at Euro Pub, one of the many cafés in the square. Did I really need a coffee after drinking Red Bull? Absolutely not. If anything, the Red Bull was kicking in, and I was starting to feel jittery. But, as so much of European life consists of sitting around and doing nothing, I decided to go with the flow. We sat down on the patio, and I ordered an Americano. A tall waitress with short blond hair and thick arms took our order.

The café was empty, but it took the waitress 20 minutes to bring the drinks. Even for Europe, this was slow. When my beverage arrived, it was lukewarm and accompanied by a cookie.

Few things in Amsterdam are free, but one such thing is the complimentary cookie served alongside coffee; or, as the Dutch say, *het koekje bij de koffie*. The tradition of serving the cookie began after World War II as a symbol of the country's wealth and financial power, and has begrudgingly continued since. The two-bite treat was an unexpected and welcome surprise. That afternoon they were serving a *bitterkoekje*, an aromatic almond macaroon defined by its plumpness. It was lovely, and tasty.

As we sipped our coffee, I made a few passing references to the oddly shaped monument in front of us. It unmistakably looked like a huge, throbbing, stone penis. Oliver, proud of his history, explained the monument was erected in the memory of Dutch soldiers in the Resistance who died in World War II. When it was unsheathed in 1956, a controversy erupted over its shape and placement feet from the district. Despite the controversy, it remained.

That night, swarms of tourists gathered around, taking pictures and striking colorful poses. Having finished my bitterkoekje, but not yet my coffee, I politely called the waitress over and asked for another.

"Huh?" she asked, confused.

"Can I please have another cookie to go with my coffee?" I repeated, pointing at my cup.

Glaring, she yelled, "You have to pay for a new coffee if you want a new cookie."

"Really?" I ask quietly. "I still have coffee left. I just need a new cookie. Just one. Can I pay for that?"

With a look of horror, and spit gathering in the sides of her mouth, she yelled, "No, I've never heard of such a thing! We don't sell cookies here. Does this look like a cookie store?" The café grew quiet as everyone watched the exchange.

"No," I said, standing up in defiance. "This does not look like a cookie store."

"So," she said, towering over me, "what's it going to be?"

We locked into a staredown. This had become personal, for both of us. I felt the Red Bull and coffee coursing through my veins, creating a chemical reaction. It felt like I was about to transform into the Hulk, or worse. My body stiffened and I began to sweat.

I am not a fighter, and have certainly never hit a lady, but these were not normal circumstances. The woman took an aggressive step in my direction. She was coming for me, all over a cookie. It was game time. Here I was thinking most Europeans were pacifists.

Realizing I was under the influence of Red Bull, and in any event, no match for this woman, I hung my head and conceded. She shook hers and scurried off, mumbling something in Dutch.

"What was that about?" I asked Oliver. "I just wanted a cookie."

"This is Holland," he said. "You'll see."

Adjusting to new cultures is never easy. Sometimes it's hard to tell when you are dealing with a cultural issue, or an asshole. I passed this one off to culture and made a mental note to never ask for an extra cookie, and when possible, lay off the Red Bull.

We finished our coffee in peace and began walking down Warmoesstraat, a narrow one-way street that led back to the station. It was also one of the pathways to the red light district. As I followed Oliver down the filthy street, I did my best to navigate around piles of dog feces that littered our path like a minefield.

Why so much shit? Holland is extremely pet friendly, and dogs are everywhere. Over 35 percent of the Dutch own a dog, resulting in over two million of them in the country—the most popular names being Luna, Max, Diesel, Bo, and Lady. They are allowed in most restaurants and on public transportation, and some say are more welcome than children. Not only is the Netherlands the only country in the world that has a political party dedicated to animals, that party has a seat in parliament. It's called the Party for the Animals, or Partij voor de Dieren. The Dutch love for animals runs strong.

As a consequence, dog crap in Amsterdam is everywhere. It's almost as if it's been strategically placed. You can find it on bridge railings, windowsills, and even an occasional bike seat. Places no dog, other than perhaps a Great Dane, could possibly crap.

At that moment, we had more pressing concerns. Hoards of tourists and junkies clogged the street, looking in random directions and seemingly oblivious to everyone around them. Avoiding physical contact was challenging, and we bounced off them like balls in a pinball machine. Unlike in New York, where you can walk down a crowded street with almost no contact, it was almost as if we were being targeted. Some even lowered their shoulders before impact, rather than attempting to steer clear.

The street was lined with youth hostels, coffeeshops, smart shops, sex shops, and kebab stands. While none of Amsterdam's windows were located on Warmoesstraat, the heart of the district lurked a few feet away. In seconds, we had gone from standing in a beautiful European square to walking in the underworld.

One smart shop, called Conscious Dreams, had a sign reading, "Magic Mushrooms—Herbal E—Cosmic Cacti—Various Herbs." Not only was weed legal in Amsterdam, or at least tolerated, hallucinogenic mushrooms, herbal ecstasy, and other psychedelics were as well.

As we paused to take in the scene, a strung-out emaciated lady with a limp lurched in front of us. She wore a torn leopard-skin top and pink spandex pants, and approached Oliver as if she knew him. Oliver froze as she stopped within inches, her breath a lethal combination of vomit and alcohol.

"Got a guilder? Got a guilder?" she asked, favoring her left leg. Oliver just stood there. She moved closer. "Got a guilder? Got a guilder?" she echoed.

Finally, Oliver got the courage to respond. "Sorry, I'm a student."

"Well," she said confidently, "I'm a princess."

"OK," Oliver replied, and we continued on our way.

Halfway down Warmoesstraat, we came across a spot called Café Hill Street Blues. With a cardboard cutout of Uncle Sam in the window, the place was calling my name. In need of a reprieve from the commotion, we walked in and ordered a beer. The place was relatively empty, and we sat by the front. We soon realized this was no ordinary bar.

Café Hill Street Blues was one of Amsterdam's 294 coffeeshops. At the time, 83 of them could also serve alcohol. Upon entering, we were presented with a menu featuring over 15 variations of marijuana and hash, including White Widow, AK-47, Super Silver Haze, Hill Street Special, Northern Lights, and Jack Herer. All classic strains. The average price for a gram was about seven guilders, or $4. Incredibly cheap compared to the United States, where you had few options. Back home, weed was weed. If you were looking to smoke, you had to be discreet and happy with whatever. In Holland, it was out in the open, and a delicacy.

Much has changed in the world with respect to cannabis, especially in California and Colorado. Back then, the scene was unique to Amsterdam and attracted millions. Say what you will about cannabis, but one thing's for sure. It has a way of bringing people together, and creating a sense of community that can transcend race, class, and, to a certain extent, politics. It can help people find the moment, the now, and stay in it. There was a stillness and beauty to it all. What you're left with is just you, and those around you. Everything else fades to the background, especially in a wonderland like Amsterdam.

Like a shrine, the walls of the coffeeshop were decorated with colorful graffiti. Everywhere you looked was a moment captured in time. The graffiti went back years. For the most part, people wrote about love, space cakes, and politics. There were warnings and words of wisdom, too.

One message read, "These walls are a testament that stupidity is international. Think before you write. Buy Jagermeister and live long."

Another warned, "Things are not as they seem. Open your eyes."

Yet another proclaimed, "We are who we want to be. Choose wisely."

I noticed a sign setting forth the bar rules. It read, "No hard drugs, no weapons, no sexual harassment, no racism, no aggression, no antisocial behavior." Rules like this only come in response to problems, and I realized the place might not be as safe as it seemed, notwithstanding Uncle Sam guarding the door. The place had its history. I surveyed the bar for signs of looming antisocial behavior. Other than a British guy in the corner aggressively picking his nose, all was clear. But I was on high alert.

Shrouded in a cloud of smoke, we watched as strangers relaxed in each other's company, rolled joints, and became lost in their thoughts.

"Want to smoke?" Oliver asked. "It's OK if you do."

"Nah, I'm good with Red Bull, coffee, wine, and beer for the night," I said, knowing my limits. "But I'll buy some for later."

I took a look at the menu and purchased two grams of Jack Herer and a gram of White Widow. I paid 20 guilders and gave the waitress an extra guilder as a showing of thanks. I knew the Dutch rarely tip. I learned that my first day, but I was still an American.

Turning to Oliver, I opened the dime bag of Jack and took a whiff.

"Ah, this is good," I said, as the smell exploded from the bag. It was a sweet, spicy, piney, skunky scent, unlike anything I had ever experienced. "You know what? Fuck it. Looks like it's time to smoke," I said. "Any good at rolling?"

"Ah, me?" Oliver replied, defensively. "I don't really smoke or hang in these places. They're mostly for tourists, not the Dutch," he said. "But go ahead."

"To each his own," I replied, and proceeded to roll a joint.

In Amsterdam, few smoke out of pipes and bongs. The Dutch roll their joints, often mixing cannabis with tobacco. I was going to do the same, minus the tobacco. It took several attempts to get it right, after licking the wrong side of the paper and doing other amateurish things. The joint wasn't pretty, but I finally nailed it, more or less.

In need of fresh air, we made our way downstairs to the lower level of the coffeeshop that overlooked a canal. There was a pool table, and Oliver asked if I wanted to play. I said sure, and we waited for two American girls to finish their game. They were smoking too, and any time one of them would sink a ball, they would yell, "ball in hole," and start kissing.

When we showed up, seven balls remained. We figured the game would be over soon. Most games would. We figured wrong. Half an hour later, the girls were still deep in it. It was getting late, and I was stoned and restless. With no end in sight, I asked Oliver if he wanted to play another time and check out the district.

"Really?" he asked, surprised.

"Sure. You've been there before, right?"

"Not really," he said. "I walked through once when I was fifteen, but just for a few seconds."

"Come on," I urged. "It's time to start my research."

Just like many New Yorkers have never visited the Statue of Liberty, and many Angelinos have never checked out Griffith Observatory, many Dutch have never toured the red light district. As Oliver followed me down Warmoesstraat, he was on edge. I was too. We made a left on Wijde Kerksteeg and found ourselves standing in front of the Oude Kerk. It was there that my journey into the district would officially begin.

The district is sprawling, covering roughly a square mile. Once inside, the rest of the world melts away. One enters a new reality. The district isn't hidden from the city, but sits in its most accessible part. One need not venture far to find it. While seemingly godless, it's home to many of Amsterdam's most beautiful structures including the Oude Kerk, Amsterdam's oldest building, built over 800 years ago and consecrated in 1306. It's also filled with apartments, cafes, bars, and even a preschool. It's a place of contrasts— where worlds collide, and have for centuries. The old church looms large over the district like a guardian, or spiritual anchor. That night it had an imposing presence, but a comforting one as well.

Prostitution has existed in Amsterdam since the sixteenth century. It was legalized in 1810. The change was based on the understanding criminalization does more harm than good. As women in windows were considered self-employed, their activities fell within the law. So, that's where most women went. All forms of exploitation, such as brothels, remained illegal for another 189 years. Since brothels didn't legally exist, they couldn't be regulated and were largely home to foreign and underage women. Once that changed, the same health and safety protections afforded women in the windows were extended to those in the brothels as well.

The origins of the term *red light district* remain unclear. Some claim it's from the early twentieth century when railroad workers used red lanterns for signaling. They would leave their lanterns outside a girl's door when visiting, indicating she was busy. Others say the term dates back to the 1890s when girls would put red shades on candles in their windows to advertise, similar to the custom today. Red light districts weren't confined to Amsterdam, but existed in 12 other Dutch cities, including Arnhem. The red light district in Amsterdam has always been the largest and most historic.

That night, I didn't wander into the old church, nor was I admiring its Gothic architecture. I certainly wasn't reflecting on the history of the place. Rather, I was reflecting on a cluster of African women in a semicircle of windows before us. Standing before them, with the church behind us, was like standing before a tribunal. Our day of judgment had come.

Wearing thongs and missing teeth, the Rubenesque women did everything they could to get our attention. All eyes were on us, and they were aggressive. For sure, there are many beautiful dark-skinned women in the district, but not here. Not by the old church. Some knocked and scratched on their windows as we passed, others stuck out their tongues. All of them were bouncing up and down, jiggling in every direction.

Despite their enthusiasm, they seemed sad and angry. We jumped back as one of them opened her door feet from us, afraid we would get dragged into their world. We walked quickly by, hoping the district would have more to offer. Oliver trailed slightly behind, trying his best to appear disinterested. It was hard not to look. One lady caught him taking a peek and flashed her pussy, pressing it up against her window.

This was the so-called *welcoming committee*. For many tourists, these are the first and last women they see. I've heard countless stories of people encountering them, only to pull a 180 and never return to the district. That night, we kept walking.

Back in 1999, the district was larger than today with over 500 windows. While just an estimate, looking back, it's safe to say about 20 percent of the women were gorgeous, 50 percent attractive, and the remaining 30 percent not-so-good. So far, we had only seen the not-so-good women. That was about to change. A few steps past the church, we found ourselves in the heart of the *De Wallen*, or *De Walletjes*, Dutch for "little walls."

The area had an oddly festive atmosphere, reminiscent of a carnival, or perhaps zoo. Despite the late hour, the streets were packed. We saw mothers pushing babies. We saw teenagers and senior citizens. We saw missionaries wearing shirts reading "Jesus Loves You," and chanting Hare Krishnas. We saw lots of men—some alone, but mostly in groups. Then we saw the women. Oliver and I were speechless. For 50 guilders, or $25, far less than dinner and a movie, you could spend 15 minutes with the girl of your dreams.

We stopped on the corner of Sint Annendwarsstraat to take everything in. In front of us was Sexyland, one of the many sex arcades in the district. Inside, people could spend a few guilders to watch videos of every possible description in the privacy of their booth. Men visited to prepare for their 15 minutes or simply take care of business, leaving sticky balls of tissue paper behind. It was a nasty place, and reverberated with the sounds of self-gratification.

Next to us stood one of Sexyland's mop-boys, taking in a breath of fresh air before returning to the stench of sex and pine-scented disinfectant that permeated the place. The guy had a job that ranked up there with the world's worst. Yet, compared to those around him, he was the lucky one. Together, the three of us listened as the chimes of the old church sounded. It was nearly midnight. As the prettiest women work late, this was prime time.

We continued walking. The street became so congested we couldn't avoid rubbing shoulders with strangers, sometimes colliding. Just like when walking down Warmoesstraat, but worse. With sex on everyone's mind, merely bumping into someone was horrifying. Moreover, many were likely loaded on herbal ecstasy, popular at the time. While on the drug, incidental contact could become a sexual high, and I did everything in my power to steer clear of the crowds. Avoiding them completely was impossible, and I often found myself standing face to face with some of the creepiest guys ever, only to sidestep out of the way.

The crowd funneled us onto a small street called Bethlemsteeg. It felt like we were being swept along by a raging river. Bethlemsteeg was no more than 10 feet wide and had a row of eight windows to our left. To our right was a cement wall. The name *Bethlem* not only reminded me of Bethlehem, the birthplace of Jesus, but also the Bethlem Royal Hospital, England's infamous insane asylum. I didn't know it at the time, but the street would play a large role in the events to come. It would either be a place I would find something divine, or be left picking up the pieces.

Unlike most of the other streets, Bethlemsteeg dead-ended after about a hundred feet. At the end of the street was a doorway, but no door. Instead, hanging from the doorframe were thick strips of plastic covered in grime. It was not a welcoming sight, and we were reluctant to enter. The current pushed us through.

Once inside, we found ourselves in a circular hallway home to nine girls. This was the La Vie en Rose, or "covered area." Techno music radiated through the dimly lit lair that reeked of cheap perfume, sex, and cleaning fluids. The plastic barrier made the air thick and heavy. It felt like being underwater. I did my best to breathe through my mouth to escape the smell, but it was inescapable. It was as if the air of a hundred years lingered in the place. It was smothering. I could just about chew it.

The red haze from the lights was intoxicating but ominous. Best way to describe it, it felt like visiting Pleasure Island from *Pinocchio* seconds before everyone turned into donkeys. There was a sense of immediacy, a feeling it might be the last night on Earth. From here the district derives much of its power. That, combined with fantasy, creates a potent cocktail, and a paradox. While there is a feeling of being transported to another time, there is also a feeling of being immersed in the now. Both happen at once. While terrifying, it was also exhilarating, and for many, highly addictive.

Some of the curtains were drawn. Most were not, and we found ourselves surrounded by a swarm of attractive women. Every girl seemed to have her own approach to doing business. One girl stood halfway out her doorway, smiling at everyone. One just winked. Another sat on a barstool, reading a magazine and talking on her cell phone. The prettiest girl was stretched out on her bed in partially unbuttoned jeans, working on a crossword puzzle. Most seemed disinterested in the men around them, heightening their appeal. For hookers, they were playing hard to get.

After a minute, the current took us full circle and spit us out onto Bethlemsteeg. The district can be overwhelming, and I was feeling the effects. The rules of society no longer seemed to apply. The place had its own code, something I knew nothing about. Oliver hadn't spoken in minutes. He just stood next to me in silence, picking his cuticles. This was his country, but the district was unlike anything he had imagined or remembered. It was worse in many respects, but also intriguing, and surreal.

The length of the street names was also surreal, making them so convoluted they were almost impossible to pronounce. This only heightened my sense of disorientation. While the Dutch use the Roman alphabet, the language often seemed as foreign as Cyrillic or Greek. Once I realized most of the streets ended with *kade*, *straat*, or *steeg*, they became a bit more manageable.

Happy to be free from the grasp of the La Vie en Rose, we made our way back to the corner of Sint Annendwarstraat and Bethlemsteeg. Once there, we proceeded down Trompettersteeg, the narrowest street in the district. Just like no trip to San Francisco is complete without a drive down Lombard Street, no trip to the district is complete without a walk down Trompettersteeg. 16 tightly packed windows line both sides of a pathway only a few feet wide, which becomes narrower as you go. Out of necessity, Oliver and I walked in a single file line. At times we had to sidestep. Once we started, there was no turning back. The crowds basically made that impossible.

The girls stood inches away on both sides of the street. We could just about feel the warmth from their bodies as we passed one beautiful girl after another who didn't seem to belong there. Almost all of them were stunning. Some made eye contact, trying to lure us in. Merely inches away, their gazes were intense and intimate. I would look away, only to be confronted by the next girl in line. Many of the women were as lifelike as department store mannequins, or perhaps wax figures from Madame Tussauds. They stood quietly behind their windows amidst cans of Red Bull and lubricating jelly, swaying back and forth.

Trompettersteeg, while intense, takes only about 30 seconds to navigate. We made our way through and found ourselves standing on the edge of a canal. Looking at the reflections on the water was refreshing. Just like New York City couldn't survive without Central Park, the same could be said about Amsterdam's canals. The city couldn't breathe without them.

As I gazed across the water, I was ready to begin. The problem was, I had no idea how to start. I had no contacts. I had no experience. I was an outsider. Every day, thousands of tourists swarm the district. Now I was one of them. The thought of building a relationship with one of these women seemed crazier than ever. They didn't come to Amsterdam for a social life. They certainly didn't come to write a book.

We ended the night in a bar called The Last Waterhole. Located off Warmoesstraat, it was a late-night hot spot. The place was packed with Americans listening to Tom Petty and drinking Heineken, and was popular for a reason. It was one of the few places in town people would go looking for action when they didn't want to pay, like your typical American bar.

Unlike in America however, where people hook up in bars all the time, randomly finding romance in Holland is difficult, if not impossible. Generally speaking, the Dutch are reserved. While a Dutch girl will be polite and entertain a chat, ask for her phone number and forget it. The request will likely be rejected or ignored. It's just not something the Dutch do. It's not how the system works. In Holland, a new relationship requires a proper introduction from family or friends, and takes time to develop. Hooking up with strangers is uncommon, unless you're hooking up with a hooker.

Oliver and I sat at a table with a candle burning in a Jack Daniel's bottle and reflected on the night. At that moment, I had only spoken with one prostitute in my life—Sarah from the Mustang Ranch. I had no idea what I was getting myself into. To say I was uneasy about things was an understatement. Shit was about to hit the fan. I could smell it.

"Still think you can write about this place?" Oliver asked.

"Don't know," I said, ambivalently. "It sounds crazy, but it's just something I need to do, for better or worse. I've felt that with my other books, too. The problem is, everything with this one is totally out of my control."

"Well," Oliver said, "when it comes down to it, isn't everything in life totally out of our control?"

"Yeah, sure," I said, too tired to get into a philosophical debate about determinism and destiny. But he had a point. I had no idea where my journey would lead, but I knew once it began, just like when walking down Trompettersteeg, there would be no turning back.

The philosopher Martin Buber explains, "All journeys have secret destinations of which the traveler is unaware." Without question, the secrets of my journey had yet to be revealed. Far from it. I could never have anticipated the events that would soon unfold, events that would forever change my understanding of the district and the women who work there.

Chapter 4

THE NEXT NIGHT Oliver and I grabbed dinner at Kam Yin, a Surinamese restaurant on the edge of the district. Suriname's ties to the Netherlands are strong, having been a Dutch colony that gained independence in 1975. Despite being the smallest country in South America, its influence was everywhere, as were the green and red flags that plastered the restaurant's façade. I had never eaten Surinamese cuisine before. Before coming to Holland, I didn't even know it existed.

The food was a peculiar mix of Indian, African, Chinese, and European cuisine, and it took time to process the menu. I selected something called a Rijst Pom Speciaal, and Oliver chose the Roti Kip Speciaal, both chicken dishes of some sort. A huge part of living abroad is ordering food and having no idea what you are getting. I could only hope I would be pleasantly surprised. When the dish arrived, it was edible, but chewy.

I picked at my meal as we observed people making their way to and from the district. As I watched a parade of prostitutes walk by, I reflected on how, for the next few minutes, they would just be normal girls walking through town. Soon, all that would change, and they would become something else. Not only externally, but likely internally, too. I wondered what that moment of transformation was like—the second a girl walks into a window and leaves the world behind.

During dinner I told Oliver how I planned to proceed. "I'll start where that narrow street was," referring to Trompettersteeg, but forgetting the name. "But I'll go everywhere if necessary. I'll knock on windows, introduce myself, and take it from there."

Oliver looked at me like I was insane. "No way. That won't work," he said, shaking his head. "This is Holland. They're only interested in money. They aren't going to care about your book."

"I think you're wrong," I said tentatively. "I'll find someone."

"You'll have to pay."

"No. I can't," I firmly replied, "and I can't have sex with any of them either. That's one rule I must follow. If I cross that line and become a customer, the book would be compromised."

Of this, I was sure. I knew for me to take readers on the journey I wanted, I could never waver. I needed to maintain my innocence. I needed to write the book from that perspective, from the reader's perspective—well, from most of their perspectives, that is. Otherwise, the book would lose its integrity, and at the time, I felt I would lose mine. I knew if

I slept with just one, it wouldn't stop there. How could it? If it was good, I would want more. If it was bad, I might want to try again. My own actions would undermine everything I was trying to accomplish. How else could I pursue a story about goodness, beauty, and self-worth? I was not willing to treat these women as commodities. They were people, not things. I felt all would be lost if I ever paid a guilder, or 50, even just to talk.

There were few rules I set for myself, but this was one I was determined to follow. This would be my challenge. This would be my path.

"Also," I continued, "if I pay them, I couldn't trust them. They would have money on their minds, not the truth. It wouldn't work. It wouldn't be genuine." I paused for a moment, and continued, "My mission is simple," I said with conviction. "I need to find a girl who wants to tell the truth, without money exchanging hands. I need to find a girl who still believes. Not only in herself, but that change is possible."

"What the hell are you talking about?" Oliver said, laughing, barely able to take me seriously. "They don't care. It's all about money." I could tell Oliver was amused by my innocence, but thought I was a fool. Typical American shit. I was looking to do something unprecedented in a place I didn't belong.

"Well, there's only one way to find out. Let's see what happens," I said.

Oliver became nervous. He had no desire to go back so soon. He thought we were just having dinner. "If it's fine with you, I think I'll go home," he replied. "I have things to do. Maybe next time."

We finished our meal and said goodbye. Soon, for the first time, I would be venturing into the district, alone. So many feelings flooded my mind—excitement, purpose, fear, uncertainty, and inevitability. It felt like there was something I needed to do, some categorical imperative. For better or worse, years of studying philosophy helped me frame the world in such light, and provided me with nothing short of a mandate. I had a job to do, and set out confident I was somewhere I was supposed to be. However, from the beginning, fate seemed to be telling me otherwise. I just didn't read the clues.

As I stepped outside, I was so eager to start my night I didn't look in both directions. The thought didn't cross my mind. It was a quiet night, and a one-way street. Suddenly I heard the sound of bells. Next, all I remember is Oliver pushing me up against a wall and a bike flying by. I felt the air move around me. A few inches closer, I would have been finished. *If I'm somewhere I'm supposed to be*, I thought, *I'm in for a rocky ride.*

"I think you just saved my life," I said, rattled.

"Yeah, maybe," Oliver casually replied.

Near misses are common in Amsterdam, as are collisions, and getting hit by a bike ranks up there with the city's greatest hazards. Throughout my stay, I saw tourist after tourist taken down hard, completely by surprise. One moment they might be walking out of a coffeeshop. The next, bam! Some even joke the only way to avoid getting hit by a bike in Amsterdam is not coming to Amsterdam. The bike is lord of the street, to which everything must yield. Thankfully, Oliver was there for me that night. From the beginning, he had my back.

Upon regaining my composure, I said goodbye to Oliver for the second time that night and continued into the district. The crowds had yet to arrive, but there were people about. I recognized some of the girls from the night before, and smiled as I passed. A few smiled back as though they recognized me too.

Going into this, all I knew was I wanted to write a book. As explained to Oliver, I had no real plan, no brilliant strategy except for putting myself out there and seeing what might happen. So far, the only thing that had happened was me almost getting run over. I knew if I wasn't careful, my journey might be over before it began. There were dangers about. I would need to discover them, and then avoid them the best I could.

While I knew my journey would be complicated, my agenda was simple. Therein lay its strength. I wanted to tell the truth. Given the purity of my intentions, I was hopeful I'd find someone who'd help. After all, I was offering a chance to set the record straight, and to restore self-worth. Idealistic, for sure. But, in my mind, that was the point. I believed there was at least one girl looking for the same. The trick was finding her.

As I roamed the district, I felt like a shy kid at his first high school dance. Every time I saw a girl, I double-clutched. I couldn't make a move. It was like I was 15 all over again.

My body froze and weighed a thousand pounds. My heart pounded as I made several laps around the district, wondering what I was doing.

Searching for strength, I remembered the first time I scouted a rapid during whitewater rafting school. We were on the South Fork of the Salmon. The water was running high. We had a choice—go down the main channel, which was treacherous, or take the easy way. We discussed our options, and the risks, and looked to our leader.

She said a few words that stayed with me. "Go big or go home. We only do this once."

Reflecting on her words, I spotted a girl on Trompettersteeg who reminded me of Sarah from the Mustang Ranch. No other men were nearby. She seemed sweet and safe. I approached. She opened her window, and said in a thick Eastern European accent, "Fityguilda fucosuc."

"Huh?" I said, caught off guard.

"Fityguilda fucosuc. Yes? Yes? You come. You come now," she frantically repeated.

"Um," I said, fumbling for words. "I'm not here for that. I'm here to write a book."

Flashing a glare, she yelled, "Fuck your book, and go fuck yourself."

Slamming her door in my face, she resumed swaying back and forth as if I didn't exist. I stood there for a few seconds, traumatized. I wasn't expecting such hostility. Apathy, yes, but not hostility. The hostility didn't end there. "Go away," she mouthed from behind her window. "You go, you go now," she screamed.

Despite my first attempt being a disaster, I wasn't ready to give up. I knew it wasn't going to be easy. Fueled by optimism, naivety, and fear, I wandered a few feet down Bethlemsteeg into the La Vie en Rose and approached my next potential collaborator. This time she was a beautiful dark-skinned girl with a twinkle in her eye. I had a good feeling about her, even better than the last.

"Fifty guilders fuck or suck," she said from behind her window, partially ajar.

"Hi. I'm David. Nice to meet you," I said, changing my approach.

"Hi, David," she said formally. "Nice to meet you too. Where are you from?"

"California," I said, excited to be building rapport.

"Nice," she said, smiling. "I was just watching *The A-Team*. You know it?"

"Yeah," I replied.

"It's my favorite," she said, beaming. "Now you must come in. We have so much in common."

"Thanks," I said, excited about our energy. "But I'm not looking for that. You seem smart, and I'm working on a book. Can we talk sometime?"

"Sorry," she said coldly, closing her door.

Next girl, same thing. This time partially in Dutch. "Fifty guilders neuken of pijpen," said a petite brunette. I didn't need a translator.

I responded, "Hey, what's up? I just moved from America. I'm a writer, and would love help with a book."

Switching to English, she continued, "Come in. Have fun. Then we talk."

"I'm not here for that," I replied, continuing in Dutch, "je bent zo mooi."

"What?" she replied, confused.

"Je bent zo mooi," I repeated, meaning, "you're so beautiful." I had just learned the phrase. It had to impress her.

It didn't. She slammed the door in my face, cussing me out from behind her window.

Still believing in my mission, I knocked on just about every window I could. It was estimated that, on any given night in 1999, there were over 6,000 prostitutes working in Amsterdam. It felt like I had been rejected by them all. After two hours of getting dissed by countless prostitutes, many of whom barely spoke English, I called it a night. It was humiliating, and I felt like a fool.

I returned several more times over the next few weeks and knocked on many more windows. While each girl looked different, the conversations were the same. Each one began with a familiar phrase, "Fifty guilders, fuck or suck." Each one ended with a door being slammed in my face, often in disgust, and usually before I could even finish a sentence. Everything seemed to indicate my plan had no chance of success. None whatsoever.

Chapter 5

WEEKS PASSED, AND I'd just about given up on the book. It was demoralizing getting rejected by prostitute after prostitute, over and over. Moreover, many of the girls now recognized me. It wasn't a good thing. They would roll their eyes, stick out their tongue, flash an areola, or make some other lovely gesture as I passed. I was not a paying customer. They knew it. My presence was unwanted. Despite my efforts, I'd made no progress. If anything, I'd made enemies. As there was little hope anything would change, I redirected my attention to the other reason I'd come to Amsterdam, the study of international law.

As an exchange student at the Vrije Universiteit, I was placed in the Master of Laws program. It was graduate school for foreign attorneys, mostly made up of lawyers from Indonesia, Germany, Holland, and America. There were also a handful from Moscow and Minsk. We came from different worlds, had different views, and weren't afraid to share them. It was our own little United Nations.

With the idea of the book no longer viable, I immersed myself in the academic community. That said, after some strategic course selection, and a bit of luck, I ended up with all my classes on Thursdays. Academically, the day was brutal. I had four 2-hour seminars in a row. But, after the long day, I would have a six-day weekend to recover. I was willing to make the sacrifice.

During the first few weeks of school, our crew became close. We studied together, drank together, and explored together. I bonded with two lawyers in particular, Indonesian Mike and German Kyle. Indonesian Mike was a wild man from Jakarta with a huge smile and big heart. German Kyle, who we affectionately called Kyle Van Damme, was hard on the outside, soft on the inside, and was all about taking care of business.

Soon, our class started taking trips. While Amsterdam is the Netherland's cultural capital, its religious and political centers are elsewhere. Places we were eager to explore. First, we traveled to Utrecht, the religious center of the Netherlands, and home to its largest university. We climbed the spiral stairs of the Dom Tower, roamed the canals, and visited the gardens. With its history dating back to the Middle Ages, Utrecht was full of depth and spirituality, and standing atop the Dom Tower was divine. We could see for miles, and the serenity provided a much-needed escape from Amsterdam.

For our next trip, as an extension of criminology class, we met our professor at the central station and traveled to The Hague, or as the Dutch say, Den Haag. This is the political center of the Netherlands. Whereas Amsterdam is the Netherland's New York, Den Haag is their Washington. I knew little about the place other than Oliver was from there.

It was a short train ride and we were there before we knew it. First, we toured the International Court of Justice. Next, we visited the Supreme Court of the Netherlands, where we spent time with sitting judges. Learning about another culture can be invaluable when trying to understand your own, and the trip provided a depth of learning no textbook could provide. More than ever, it felt right being in Holland. I had already begun seeing the world with new eyes.

Having visited the spiritual and political capitals of the Netherlands, there was only one more capital to explore. This one would require a passport. While dancing at a nightclub to the song "Blue" by Eiffel 65, Indonesian Mike, German Kyle and I made a last-minute decision. At three o'clock in the morning, we set out on a road trip. Our destination was Oktoberfest, the biggest beer festival in the world.

With no change of clothes, Indonesian Mike and I piled in the back of Kyle's Audi and took off down the autobahn at speeds exceeding a hundred miles an hour. The drive was exhilarating. With the help of Red Bull and two bathroom breaks, we arrived in Munich fully charged, relieved, and ready to go.

Oktoberfest is made up of massive beer-drinking tents the size of football fields. Most have strict guest lists. We had no reservations. German Kyle was unfazed. He had done this before. He was a professional. He was Kyle Van Damme.

He approached one of the tents and stated his name. When his name didn't appear on the list, he threw a fit, yelling, "*Da muss ein Irrtum vorliegen*," over and over. I learned this meant, "There must be some mistake." In the commotion, he grabbed the guest list and pretended to look for his name, which he insisted was there, but wasn't. While doing so, he memorized another name on the list. We went to a different door, used the name, and bingo, we were in.

The strategy gained us access to the biggest tents such as Schottenhamel, Augustiner, and Hofbräu. Once inside Hofbräu, Indonesian Mike and I were so excited we purchased matching Hofbräuhaus hats. They were the ultra-touristy kind, made from gray felt and shaped like a triangle. German Kyle refused to wear one. It was his country, he said. He had a reputation to uphold.

Now with access to the tents and dressed to the nines, it was time to party. The next 48 hours were spent drinking beer, making friends, eating pretzels, singing, dancing, waiting for the bathroom, and, finally, sleeping in our car. We tried to find a place to stay, but the hotels were booked. We made the best of it, and had no problem passing out.

Of all the challenges we faced, the bathroom situation was the worst. The lines were interminable. They took hours. With people cutting everywhere, those patiently waiting, including us, were suckers. It was a war zone. Many Oktoberfest veterans would skip the bathrooms altogether, opting to discretely pee in an empty stein under their table. This was common practice, especially for the Germans, and Kyle warned us to never accept a stray beer from a stranger.

We took Kyle's advice and our trip was more or less incident free, except for one thing. With a few hours to go before heading home, Indonesian Mike and I were wandering the grounds, minding our business, doing what you do at Oktoberfest. As always, Mike was smoking his Indonesian clove cigarettes and we were wearing our Hofbräu hats, high-fiving strangers. German Kyle lagged behind, intentionally.

Suddenly, we heard the sounds of aggressive German. We turned around, figuring it was a drunken fool. We figured wrong, and found ourselves face to face with two police officers. They were gesturing at the burning cigarette and screaming, their German shepherds barking in unison.

"Marijuana," they yelled, louder and louder, pointing at the cigarette.

"No, cloves. Just cloves," Indonesian Mike replied.

"Marijuana," they repeated.

"No, Indonesian cigarettes! Cloves. They are cloves!" my friend pleaded, now shaking.

The Germans were convinced it was marijuana. There was nothing we could do about it. Obviously, they were not familiar with Indonesian culture, or the smell of weed. With German Kyle nowhere to be found, all we could do was say, "cloves," and "Indonesian cigarettes," again and again. One of the officers grabbed Mike by the arm and reached for the cigarette. I was convinced he was about to get arrested. Maybe I would, too, just because—German tyranny at its worst. Luckily, German Kyle caught up with us and cleared the confusion. They reluctantly released Mike, but only after confiscating his supply.

With the police gone, Kyle laughed as he reflected on us almost crapping our pants. Fuck him, though, as that was some scary shit. Other than that, it was basically your standard trip to Oktoberfest. Kyle even taught us some German along the way, including *du bist so hübsch* and *ich liebe München*. Meaning, "you're so pretty," and, "I love Munich." The locals loved it.

For two days, Mike, Kyle, and I started drinking at 10 o'clock in the morning and lasted until 10 at night. We were the perfect trio. An American, a German, and an Indonesian, three brothers-in-arms for the weekend, creating moments that would last forever. After drinking countless steins of beer, we jumped back on the autobahn and headed home. Mike and I wore our Hofbräu hats the entire way, waving at cars, Kyle shrugging behind the wheel.

While this was going on, my colleagues at Berkeley were studying esoteric electives in a stifling library, worrying about their future. It felt good to be free from the paranoia. I had separated from the pack, at least temporarily. I remembered when the dean tried to convince me to stay.

"But I'll be taking classes there," I said.

"Yes, David, but not at Berkeley Law," she said condescendingly. "There's only one Berkeley Law." Higher education is as much about control as anything else. I had left their jurisdiction.

That is not to say I was taking time off academically. The semester comprised a lot more than field trips. One night after a long day at university, I grabbed drinks with Kyle and Mike at Dante Kitchen & Bar. It would soon become one of our regular spots, located centrally on the Spuistraat. A group of Indonesian and Dutch students joined too, along with an American from the East Coast.

Time floated by as we drank Grolsch beer, smoked clove cigarettes, and discussed the three P's: politics, pot, and prostitution. Hours before, we had sat through a lecture on prostitution, having been assigned readings from Andrea Dworkin and Catharine MacKinnon. Given my recent experiences in the district, and disdain for academics spouting crap, I found the readings particularly interesting.

We learned Dworkin believes, "When men use women in prostitution, they are expressing a pure hatred for the female body . . . It is a contempt so deep that a whole human life is reduced to a few sexual orifices." While I had much to learn, everything I already experienced seemed to contradict her thesis. Prostitution seemed to have little to do with contempt, but everything to do with fantasy, and the desire for a no-strings-attached sexual experience. Could it really be that, each night, the men who roamed the district harbored a deep hatred for the female form? Nothing seemed further from the truth. The only contempt seemed to be coming from Ms. Dworkin herself.

MacKinnon, another critic, writes, "Now we are supposed to believe, in the name of feminism, that the choice to be fucked by hundreds of men for economic survival must be affirmed as a real choice . . . In prostitution, women are tortured through repeated rape and in all the more conventionally recognized ways. Women are prostituted precisely in order to be degraded and subjected to cruel and brutal treatment without human limits; it is the opportunity to do this that is exchanged when women are bought and sold for sex."

Like Dworkin, MacKinnon's understanding of things seemed flawed, hyperbolic, and overly simplistic. Did she really believe none of the women in Amsterdam chose to become prostitutes? Her claim that prostitution is inherently exploitive and a form of slavery, rather than a form of sexual self-determination, seemed little more than a condescending belief prostitutes don't know what they're doing and need an Ivy League elitist, like MacKinnon, to protect them.

With the subject fresh in our minds, it incited debate. Drinking my beer while picking apart a Heineken coaster, I sat and listened as an American girl in our program argued with a Dutch girl about the state of prostitution in Amsterdam, and beyond.

"When it's legal, it becomes so much easier for girls to do it," the American said. "It's immoral. Society shouldn't condone it."

"Who said laws should reflect society's values? The right to do something doesn't mean that thing is right. By legalizing alcohol, are we saying drinking is moral? No, we're simply recognizing that by outlawing it, we're doing more harm than good." Taking a sip of beer, the Dutch girl continued, "Just because something is morally wrong doesn't mean it should be illegal."

"I can't believe you said that," the American replied, rolling her eyes. "Sure it does. By allowing prostitution, we corrupt society. It spills out onto our streets," she groaned.

"That's only true when it's illegal. Look at Amsterdam. Prostitution is confined to certain areas. If you don't like it, stay away."

The American had now become emotional. The debate had become personal. Emotion hijacked reason, and dissent from her point of view was not to be tolerated. "When it comes down to it, prostitutes hurt women everywhere, including me," the American continued. "They should be condemned. It's demeaning."

"What good would that do? If anything, doesn't condemning them make the problem worse?" the Dutch girl asked. "Are you saying anything demeaning to women should be outlawed? The list would be long and include erotic dancing, and being a lawyer too," she said laughing. "But seriously, shouldn't women be able to express themselves sexually? Why can't a woman make her own choice about what she does with her body? Isn't that what the women's movement is all about?"

"That's just it. They are not making their own choices. They're victims. Only the most vulnerable become prostitutes."

"Anyone who compels a woman to become a prostitute should be punished," the Dutch girl said, acknowledging her point. "But that's different from punishing someone who chooses to become one. You call them victims, but didn't we learn about several women's groups who view them as liberated? The better question is, how can we stop them? Prostitutes have been around for thousands of years. If a woman wants to sell her body for sex, she'll do it, anywhere and anytime. By arresting them, you only give them a criminal record and make it harder for them to return to society."

"I still think it's immoral," the American continued.

"Well, according to whose morals? I respect what you believe to be immoral. You have your beliefs, and that's fine. But why should the law reflect your morals as opposed to mine? Especially if by doing so, we sacrifice the health and safety of women who, for whatever reason, are drawn into the profession. This has nothing to do with morals, but finding practical solutions to real problems."

"What happens when they get old? How do they support themselves? It costs society in the end. It's a dead-end job."

"Well, so is professional athletics," the Dutch girl interrupted. "Do we also want to ban that?"

"I'm done," the American proclaimed. Tension filled the air. The two women sat across from each other, motionless.

Speaking for the first time, I asked the American, "Have you ever even been to the district?"

"I would never go there," she coldly replied.

"I have and would again," the Dutch girl said. The Indonesians, who had yet to check out the scene, expressed interest too.

Exhausted from the conversation, I said, "You know what, after drinks, why don't we all go? I know my way around."

Soon, I was once again walking down Warmoesstraat, this time leading a parade of Indonesians and a Dutch girl. We walked in a close pack, gaining strength in each other's company. The American didn't come. I tried to convince her, but she told me to fuck off. German Kyle didn't make it either. It had been weeks since I was last in the district. For some reason, it felt good to be on my way back.

Chapter 6

THE 11 O'CLOCK chimes of the old church rang as we made our way into the district. The streets were crowded and it was raining, but not enough to dare open an umbrella—not in Holland, where umbrellas are reserved for serious weather. A thick mist consumed the streets, making the district more mysterious than ever. In order to navigate through the tourists, johns, and junkies, the group walked behind me in a single file line. I felt like a tour guide in a theme park, the only thing missing being a stick with a flag on it.

Conversation ceased as we strolled past a few women. The group grew more uncomfortable with every step. Standing alongside a canal, we momentarily stopped to regroup. I then nonchalantly directed everyone to follow me down Trompettersteeg. They looked at me like I was crazy.

"Is that even a street?" one of them asked. They had gone far enough.

It was only after some persuading they changed their minds. I convinced them it was an educational experience. One by one, they made their way through the claustrophobic passage, doing their best to avoid eye contact with the girls standing inches away. It had been a while since I was last in the district and many of the faces were new, but not all of them. None of the girls seemed to remember me, and merely made standard solicitations as I passed.

Caught in the momentum of the crowd, I walked slightly ahead of the group down Bethlemsteeg in the direction of the La Vie en Rose. I figured I would take them through the covered area, and call it a night. That would be enough.

I thought everyone was following close behind. I was wrong. One of the girls became anxious and was on the brink of a panic attack. She froze like a statue. Another, wearing open-toe sandals, stepped in a puddle and screamed. Rather than follow me down Bethlemsteeg, the group stopped 10 feet away, waiting for me to return and escort them home. They were ready to leave.

Then I saw her. The first thing I noticed were her eyes. They were brown and innocent, like a deer. Despite men passing by, our eyes remained locked. It made no sense, but we seemed to recognize each other. We maintained eye contact as I approached her window. It felt like I was stuck in a tractor beam. I had no idea what I was going to say. I was unprepared and off my game. She stood around five feet eight inches tall, slightly shorter than me, and had long brown hair and a perfect figure. Seemingly European and in her early twenties, she was dressed humbly for her profession, wearing a pink mini-skirt and white lace bra. She opened her door and looked at me, saying nothing.

"Hi, I'm David," I said hesitantly.

"Hi, I'm Emma," she said with a Dutch accent. By now, I had knocked on countless windows and had been rejected every time. The book barely lingered in my mind.

Spontaneously, I said, "I just moved to Amsterdam. I'm looking to make friends. Want to grab coffee sometime?"

Emma flashed a smile and laughed. "I'm sorry," she said, touching my arm. "I'm a prostitute. I can't meet for free. If you want to meet outside my window, it's four hundred guilders an hour. What do you think?"

Momentarily forgetting I was talking to a prostitute, I said, "Come on, I can tell there's something special between us."

Again, Emma laughed, this time louder. "There's something special between me and every guy who pays fifty guilders. If you don't want to pay, I have to get back to work."

Emma was a professional. It was all business. She was just like the others. She had no desire to make it personal. That said, she continued standing with her door open, gazing into my eyes.

"I'm working on a book. I could use your help," I said.

"Great," she said, pushing up against me.

Without thinking, I said, "je bent zo mooi," and followed with, "any guy would be lucky to have a girl like you."

"You don't need luck in Amsterdam," she said tenderly, "just fifty guilders."

"Let's grab coffee. What's five minutes? I'll make it worth your while."

"Oh, is that so?" she said flirtatiously. "I'm sorry, that's my personal time. I've always wanted to be in a book, but that's impossible. This is Amsterdam. Sure you don't want to come in?"

"No, I'm not," I said, overwhelmed by the moment. "But I'm here to write a book."

Bathing in the red lights, Emma said no more. The conversation had run its course. She stepped behind the glass and closed her door. I stood there, in shutdown mode. Emma was just another working girl, same old story. Another Amsterdam hooker. But something was different.

From the time we're little, we're taught we have five senses. Hearing, sight, smell, touch, and taste. I don't believe that. That's just what they teach us. I believe there are more. Sometimes we just know things, or feel things, we can't explain. It happens to all of us. It doesn't happen every day, but it happens. My connection with Emma was one of those things. It was real. Something inside me was triggered, and I was glowing.

My friends watched from afar. They couldn't hear what we were saying, but could tell it was intense. They could tell something happened. I returned to the group and filled them in.

By the time I finished, we all needed a drink. We also needed to leave the district. I led the group down Warmoesstraat in the direction of The Last Waterhole. I had a nice time with Oliver there a few weeks ago. It was right around the corner.

As we made our way down the street, I couldn't get Emma out of my mind. In fact, with every step, it felt like I was moving in the wrong direction. As we approached the bar, a Japanese man walked by with a bucket of red roses. He tried selling some to our group. We kept walking, but it struck me as odd. I had never seen anyone selling roses in the district. It wasn't the place for romance.

Unexpectedly, I stopped in my tracks. Without realizing what I was doing, I called him over.

"How much for all the roses?" I asked.

"All of them?" the man asked, confused.

"All of them," I replied.

After doing the math, he said, "Fifty guilders."

I bought him out. Every single rose. He smiled and gave me a pat on the back. His night was made. He also seemed proud of me, as if he knew something, or saw something, I didn't.

Without saying more, I took off running to Emma's window. With water from the roses dripping down my arm, the world moved in slow motion as my perspective switched from first person to third. It felt like I was watching myself in a movie, one that no one else in the world would ever see but me. In that moment, what inspired me to buy the roses wasn't anything more than not wanting my movie to suck. I was not going to walk past the moment. There had been many times in my life I'd done just that, walked past a moment, only to have it lost forever. That night, for some reason, I wasn't going to let that happen. It wasn't out of bravery, but necessity.

It wasn't easy running over cobblestones cradling long-stemmed roses, and I almost wiped out along the way. I knew I had to get there fast or Emma might be gone, or busy. When I arrived, her curtain was open, and she was standing where I left her. A crowd had gathered. Out of breath and shaking, I walked up to her window and held out the flowers.

For a second, she just stood there. She seemed confused, and needed time to process what was going on. Finally, she moved toward her window and opened the door. Emma took the flowers, smelled them, and leaned forward to kiss my cheeks. Three times.

"You just bought yourself five minutes," she said plainly. "Meet me here tomorrow at seven." Without saying more, she escorted a man into her room and drew the curtain.

Chapter 7

THE NEXT MORNING I went to Oliver's room to tell him the news. He opened his door eating a piece of toast with sprinkles, a Dutch delicacy, and listened in disbelief.

"That's impossible," he said. "A prostitute would never just meet someone for coffee, especially a Dutch girl. She's up to something. You bought her flowers? You need to be careful. I should come with you."

I thanked him for his concern, but said I would be meeting Emma alone. This was between the two of us. For some reason, I felt I could trust her.

The day was spent in anticipation. Emma existed in a forbidden world. I was about to enter it. Although I was just grabbing coffee with a girl, the meeting had greater significance.

For most of us, we are born into a life situation that becomes the platform upon which we live our lives. Like all platforms, our life situation has boundaries, enforced by the society in which we live. The boundaries are both invisible and real, and shape how we live, and with whom we share our lives. In a few hours, I was about to step out of my life situation, and into the wilderness.

Fyodor Dostoevsky wrote about something called the burden of freedom. He explained that there is a burden existing outside the box, and stepping into the wilderness. As a result, many only feel free when they are in chains, living by society's rules and stuck within its boundaries. But they are not free at all. In *The Grand Inquisitor*, Dostoevsky writes, "Man is tormented by no greater anxiety than to find someone quickly to whom he can hand over that great gift of freedom with which the ill-fated creature is born." The sad thing is, those who refuse to hand over their freedom are often ostracized, as they force others to come to terms with their choice of surrendering theirs, all the while living the fantasy they are free. When someone lives outside the box, it challenges those who live within it. It forces them to acknowledge the box even exists.

Society's grip is powerful, especially for those who have never lived outside it. This is why traveling, and living abroad, can be so important. Trying to understand the concept of freedom when one has never lived outside one's community is like a fish trying to understand the concept of water. They are surrounded by it, so it's impossible to see. It's impossible to comprehend. It's all they know. When you live abroad, you gain perspective. You are distanced from a world once believed absolute. The grip of groupthink loosens, and the world is presented for what it is, a place of endless possibilities, where most limitations are self-imposed.

This is why many Americans who live abroad never come back. They never want to lose perspective. Once lost, it's harder than ever to recover. The shackles are tightened. The simple act of having coffee with Emma was nothing less than an act of defiance—an escape from the shackles to which I was tethered. With law school graduation months away, it was an assertion of my freedom, a declaration I was not willing to submit. Perhaps I was being a bit dramatic, but it was some intense shit.

It was a picturesque autumn day when I set out to meet Emma. There wasn't a cloud in the sky. Regardless, I grabbed my umbrella. I already learned no matter how perfect the weather, you always had to prepare for rain. In Holland, everything can change in a heartbeat.

Making sure not to be late, I arrived 30 minutes early. With time on my hands, I took a stroll through the streets. Unlike the festive atmosphere at night, the mood at dusk was somber. With the day shift ending and the night shift yet to begin, the crowds were gone and many of the windows were shut. Signs hung where women once stood, reading *kamers te huur*, or "rooms for rent." It felt like walking around a college campus during spring break. The hype and energy was gone. All that was left was the reality of the streets.

With 15 minutes to go, I walked into a bar called the Old Sailor and ordered a Heineken. Perched on the corner of Molensteeg and Oudezijds Achterburgwal, it provided some of the best panoramas of the district. This was where many tourists would pass time when their buddies were being entertained by local talent. It was a waiting room of sorts, reminiscent of a British pub. I drank my beer while leaning against a statue of the old sailor, and then made my way to Bethlemsteeg.

Emma's curtain was closed when I arrived. It was seven o'clock. I waited with my back against the dirty wall, worried she had forgotten, or worse, changed her mind. Other than a few men roaming about, I was more or less alone. When the bells of the old church sounded again, I had given up hope. As I was getting ready to leave, a girl walked by and stopped a few feet away. She wore a black leather coat, platform shoes, and tight black pants. Her hair was in a ponytail. It was Emma. She hadn't forgotten.

"Hi, David," she said cautiously. She seemed less comfortable talking to me on the streets than in her window. "I only have a few minutes. Let's go."

Emma and I walked around the corner and sat on the patio of a café called Lunch Room 52, across from the old church. The place was empty except for a sketchy dude with a mustache. He sat by himself wearing a black trench coat and open-toe sandals. He reminded me of one of the nihilists from *The Big Lebowski*, which had just been released, and wouldn't stop staring at me. I did my best to ignore him as Emma lit a cigarette, disappeared, and returned with two cups of coffee. I offered her money. She refused.

"Don't be stupid," she said, as I pushed a few guilders in her direction. "So, what's this book thing about?"

I told Emma about my background and other things one might mention when applying for a job, or going on a first date. At times, she seemed interested. At other times, bored. Throughout it all she was reserved, studying me, trying to figure out what role I might play in her life.

"So far, no one is willing to help," I said. "Many think once a girl steps behind a window, she's no longer human. I want to change that."

"You're crazy," she said. "But I'll think about it. What's in it for me?"

"The chance to demystify the profession," I said, "and make a new friend."

Emma burst out laughing. "Oh, David," she explained, "I'm not sure. I still don't see what's in it for me." With that, she opened her organizer, ripped off a page, and wrote her home phone number in black eyeliner. "Call me tonight at eleven. I'll think about it."

As we were getting up, I handed her a copy of my book on British politics, written while I was working in the House of Commons. Without comment, she took it, glanced at the picture of Harold Wilson on the cover, and slid it into her purse. I had no expectation she would read it, but at least she would know I was published, and serious about my intentions.

Like so many women who work in the district, Emma didn't live in Amsterdam. She commuted. She didn't want her professional and personal lives to mix. Since she was heading home for the night, we walked together to the central station. Out of nowhere, a bike raced by and almost ran us over. Emma saw it coming and pushed up against me, nearly forcing me into a heaping pile of dog shit. She thought it was hilarious. I wasn't quite as amused. This was now the second time I'd almost been run over, on the same street. With any luck, there wouldn't be a third.

As we continued walking in silence, I reached to hold her hand. It felt like the natural thing to do, especially after our near-death experience, or what felt like one. It was more a reflexive response than an intentional act. It surprised Emma, who released my hand after giving it a gentle squeeze.

A midget playing Sonny and Cher on a cheap keyboard serenaded us as we approached the station. I found unusual comfort in Emma's presence as we passed under the Gothic Renaissance façade and took the escalator to the tracks. No one would have guessed I was walking with a prostitute. In that moment, she was just a normal girl. A face in the crowd.

Within minutes, Emma's train came and she was gone. In no hurry, I sat down on a bench and watched as trains came and went from the station. By the time I headed out, the rain was coming down hard. I opened my umbrella and made my way down Haarlemmerstraat, randomly stopping in a coffeeshop to buy a slice of space cake. I took a bite and arrived home cold and wet, but in a nice state of mind. While my long walks home were lovely, I knew it was finally time to get a bike. That would be next on my list.

Once back in my room, I took another bite of cake and watched the rain fall on the canal. Eventually, I called Emma as promised. She picked up after one ring. It was as if she was waiting.

"I'll do it," she said. "Why not?"

"Great. Let's grab dinner Friday," I replied.

"Fine," Emma said. "Meet me at the same place, same time."

I had broken through.

Chapter 8

THERE'S A SAYING in Amsterdam that largely holds true, and it goes like this. There are two kinds of people in town—those who have had their bike stolen, and those who will. It's well known that if you buy a fancy new bike, you will likely be looking for another one in days, if not hours. Inga had said as much on my first night. When it came to getting a bike, the shittier the better.

There were several bike shops in town, but paying top dollar for a bike that would soon go missing was a raw deal. Instead, locals would meet up with junkies in the center of town near the Koningsplein and place orders for so-called used ones. This had been going on for years, and was something of a Dutch tradition. With more bikes in Amsterdam than residents, there was no lack of supply.

The action happened late at night, and the orders could be specific. Where they got the bikes, no one cared. Not even the police. Even if the police wanted to enforce the law, bike theft was an age-old problem in Amsterdam that wasn't about to be solved anytime soon.

Several weeks into my stay, I was in need of a bike. My long walks down Haarlemmerstraat in the rain made that painfully clear. Finally, I mustered up the courage to buy one. Dutch style.

After a spaghetti carbonara dinner, Oliver and I made our way to the Koningsplein. It was time to get some wheels. We stopped on a bridge and were approached by a junkie, or as they call themselves, a businessman.

He asked what we needed.

I replied, "A good one."

We paced back and forth for 15 minutes, during which time a cop pedaled by. Convinced I was about to get arrested, or worse, I looked for ways to escape. Oliver laughed and told me not to worry, but the whole thing made me uncomfortable. Eventually, the businessman came pedaling down the street on a shiny purple mountain bike. He pedaled past us, made a few circles, and returned. My bike had arrived. After a successful test drive, I purchased the thing for 25 guilders. The bike had been around the block, but had 10 speeds and a paint job. It even had a basket. Everything was great except one thing. It was a woman's bike. That said, I wasn't about to be picky. By Amsterdam standards, it was a gem.

In Amsterdam your bike becomes an extension of self, so personal people name them. I affectionately named mine the Purple Rocket. Due to its reddish tint, Oliver loved calling it the Red Rocket. I wasn't cool with that. What I really wasn't cool with, though, was the thought of it getting stolen. I was determined to prove the age-old saying wrong and not be stripped of my baby. Accordingly, the next day I purchased over a hundred guilders' worth of locks, chains, and clamps to protect a bike worth a quarter that. Such was life in Holland.

Ever since meeting Emma, I hadn't been able to think about much else. It wasn't just because of the book. She seemed willing to trust me. I didn't want to screw that up. I didn't want to let her down. Given that I wasn't paying for her time, I felt I should at least get her something as a token of my appreciation, a basic gesture of respect.

Halfway down Haarlemmerstraat, I came across a jewelry store. I knew buying Emma jewelry was a bold move. Nevertheless, I was all about it. The first order of business was finding a secure place to lock my bike. Still new to things, it took five minutes. It was all about finding the perfect location, and required a trained eye. Also, securing the back wheel clamp was a bitch.

With the Purple Rocket secured, I made my way into the store. Besides roses, I had never bought anything for a prostitute. A necklace caught my eye. It was a silver pendant, dotted with three red stones.

"You're going to make some girl happy with that," the manager said. "She must be special."

I nodded, made the 60 guilder purchase, and was on my way. I arrived at Lunch Room 52 a few minutes early and locked my bike up next to the church. It started raining and I waited inside. There were six tables in the café, all of which were empty. I sat by a window with a view of my bike for safekeeping, and listened to the seven o'clock chimes of the old church.

While looking for Emma, I studied everyone who passed, paying particular attention to the Dutch sense of style. As a whole, the Dutch were tall and thin, and most of their clothes looked shrunken, a size or two too short. It was almost as if they'd grown a foot overnight and didn't bother changing their wardrobe. They just squeezed in and carried on. I also noticed the Dutch wore pleather, and seemed to fancy colored pants, particularly red. I, on the other hand, was wearing blue jeans and a gray sweatshirt. I looked like a tourist right off the boat.

As I gazed at the church, three women and a Middle Eastern man entered the café. Two of the girls wore pleather pants. The other wore a cotton miniskirt that had a mind of its own, creeping up her thigh. The women were distracting, but my attention was focused on finding Emma, and keeping an eye on my bike. They were prostitutes, exchanging stories about their day's work.

"So this one American couldn't get it up," remarked the girl in the skirt. "Then, he asked me to marry him. He wanted to save me."

"I had two proposals today," another said. "How about you?"

"None so far, but the night is young," the third girl replied, laughing.

The man sat disinterested. After a few cigarettes, the girls stood up, took a few rolls of toilet paper from a shelf, and disappeared. The chimes of the old church sounded again. Still, no sign of Emma.

For the next hour I sat alone in Lunch Room 52. A few times I thought I saw her. I was wrong. I finally left and pedaled to a coffeeshop on Herengracht and sat for another hour, smoking Jack Herer and gazing at the silver necklace in my hand. Despite weighing a few grams, it felt like a ton. I felt like a chump. This was not how I imagined the night would go. I had been stood up by a prostitute. Worse yet, I worried I might never see her again.

Chapter 9

THE NEXT DAY I left a message on Emma's answering machine. I waited for the phone to ring. It didn't. Ever. Gazing at the canal, I felt far from home. I also felt alone, and overcome with self-doubt. How could she stand me up? Why would she say yes, and not come? At the end of the day, was I just like all the other guys in the district who thought they were special? Who thought the girl actually cared? This, after all, is what they sell. The fantasy. I bought it, hook, line, and sinker.

I took the necklace and opened the door to my balcony. Standing in the cold air, I dangled it over the rail, angry with myself for getting caught up in my emotions. I should have known better. What was I doing buying a necklace for a prostitute anyway? Looking out over the canal, I leaned back and threw the necklace as far as I could. It made a splash 50 feet away and disappeared into the water, never to be seen again. *Fuck it*, I thought. *What's the point? She didn't deserve it anyway.*

There I was, mourning the end of a relationship that never even happened. The feeling of loss was inexplicable, but real. I had come close to making a connection, only to have it slip away. Days passed, and I left more messages. I tried to stay positive, but the results were the same.

The next week was spent writing papers for criminal law, eating fries with mayo, touring the Anne Frank House, drinking Grolsch beer, and smoking cannabis. Mostly Jack Herer, White Widow, and Northern Lights. Life was back to normal, Amsterdam normal. The book was an afterthought. To my surprise, so was sex. Mostly, that is.

For many guys, especially in their twenties, life consists largely of the constant pursuit of getting laid. It's sad and crude, but true. As animals, we're programmed this way. It's a biological imperative. The species depends on it, and the pursuit hasn't been easy. Finding a mate has been competitive. This has strengthened the biological resolve, in many ways enslaving men in the process. Studies have shown that, on average, men think about sex hundreds of times a day. While that might sound groovy to some, it can be overwhelming and consuming.

When you live in a city where you can have sex with any number of beautiful women anytime you want, for $25, something changes on an evolutionary level. With such easy access, even if one doesn't indulge, the pursuit ends. There's no glory in the conquest. There's no chase. The mind is allowed to go elsewhere.

Where it goes depends on the person. For some, it's basic supply-and-demand economics. With a never-ending supply, demand dissipates. The curve flattens. The biological imperative wanes. The necessity and urgency for sex fades. For others, it's the opposite. Their mind goes into overload and unleashes a veritable feeding frenzy. The phenomenon is similar to what happens to many guys on the Internet, through sites such as match.com and others like it. They just can't get enough. Women become disposable. I was in the first category. With sex everywhere, it was no big deal. I wasn't in the hunt.

The way nudity was treated in Amsterdam was also different. Life didn't revolve around trying to get a peek. This cultural difference extended beyond the district and into the day-to-day fabric of the city itself.

During my first week in town, I joined a gym called Squash City. I heard good things about the place, and it was a short pedal from Planciusstraat. It was exactly what I was looking for. After some cardio and weights, I checked out the Roman-themed relaxation area. If this was the men's area, I could only imagine what the women's was like. It was incredible.

The place was deserted when I arrived. I took off my clothes, wrapped a towel around my waist, and hit the sauna. I poured water and eucalyptus oil on the stones and closed my eyes. The place heated up fast. Soon, I was in full sweat and relaxed as can be. I removed my towel and made myself at home.

Ten minutes into my sweat, the door opened. I had just poured water on the stones and the room was thick with steam. I couldn't see a thing. That changed, and I found myself alone with a beautiful woman. My heart pounded. What was going on? Was I in the women's area? Holy shit. The woman didn't flinch. She took off her towel and stretched out in front of me, completely naked. She then proceeded to do yoga as drops of sweat formed on her chest and rolled down her side.

We never talked, but I was in no hurry to leave. After sweating more than I thought possible, I jumped into the icy plunge pool, lasted a few seconds, and found a chair on the balcony overlooking the city. To say I felt rejuvenated would be an understatement. This was Holland. Nudity and sex were just part of life, and I was living it. Boundaries were being redefined all around me. Everything was great and in sync, except one thing. Emma haunted me.

Weeks after my last message, I biked to the district to see if she was around. Since we last spoke, Emma had likely slept with hundreds of guys. She certainly wasn't thinking about me, or the book. Halfway there, I almost decided to forget it. She stood me up. She didn't return my calls. I didn't need to be a rocket scientist to figure out what was going on. She didn't want to see me. Something compelled me to keep going. Not in the mood to spend five minutes locking up the Purple Rocket, I walked the bike through the narrow streets, getting an occasional glare along the way.

It was six o'clock, and the streets were quiet. Most of the curtains were drawn. I took my usual path, walking down Sint Annendwarsstraat and turning right on Bethlemsteeg. I didn't expect to see Emma, yet there she was, standing in her window bathed in neon. She was wearing a schoolgirl outfit, and she was holding my book.

I leaned my bike against the cement wall and waited. At first, she didn't see me. She just stood there, flipping through the pages. She was using the book as a prop. A man wearing a suit approached. I heard the usual "Fifty guilders, fuck or suck," and they reached an agreement. Just as he was about to enter, Emma saw me and called my name. Without thinking, I left my bike unattended and hurried over.

Emma kissed my cheeks three times. They weren't American kisses, but Dutch air kisses. The same kind she gave me weeks ago. Air kissing is a Dutch formality reserved for friends and family. It wasn't something you saw much of in the district. When Emma went in for the first kiss, I was flustered. So much so I leaned in the wrong direction, nearly causing a collision.

"David, it's you," she said. "Don't be mad. I had to work in a different window, and lost your number. I thought I'd never see you again."

Not sure what to think, I said, "No worries. I'm glad I found you. Want to grab dinner?"

"Look, I'm really busy, but I'm free Monday between shifts."

"Great," I said.

"I'll see you at seven," she replied, as the man in the suit lurked nearby. His interest in Emma hadn't dissipated. As I walked toward the Purple Rocket, he walked toward her. Just before Emma let him in and drew her curtain, she waved goodbye, staring emotionlessly down the street.

Chapter 10

WHEN I WOKE up Monday I was excited, but I wasn't ready to meet Emma just yet. In preparation for our date, business meeting, or whatever, I had to run a few errands.

Top on my list was returning to the jewelry store and buying Emma a new necklace. The last one was resting on the bottom of a canal. Emma had already put me through a bit of an emotional roller coaster. I was feeling vulnerable, more than I should have. But I didn't mind. In fact, part of me enjoyed being exposed. It had been a while. I returned to the store on Haarlemmerstraat and found an identical piece. No need to change things up. Mission accomplished.

Next, I needed to go clothing shopping. My only nice outfit was a Brooks Brothers shirt and pair of slacks. It didn't seem appropriate for our date. I was never one for fashion, and the thought of shopping in a foreign country was daunting. I had no choice. I knew it was time to go Dutch.

I pedaled to the stores around Dam Square to see what I could find. Notwithstanding the fact I was fashion-challenged, my main problem stemmed from the fact the Dutch are thin and lanky. I have an athletic build, weigh around 175 pounds on a good day, and am just under six feet. Wanting to fit in, both literally and figuratively, I tried on pairs and pairs of pleather pants.

The pants were tight, very tight. After several failed attempts, and nearly busting a few seams, I found a pair I could sit down in that didn't show off my ballsack. Those were my two requirements, not easy to satisfy. Happy to have found a pair that did the trick, I popped a squat to make sure all was in order and completed the purchase. To round things out, I picked up a synthetic black shirt, a gray pleather jacket, and black buckle shoes.

It was now time for the last thing on my list. The thing I dreaded most of all. It was time for a haircut. I stumbled into a barbershop on Planciusstraat and hoped for the best. The place was empty except for two North African barbers chain-smoking out front. They were engaged in a heated conversation of some sort. The older of the two jumped to attention and ushered me in. Once seated and covered, he dropped a weathered look-book in my lap and gestured for me to select a style. I flipped through the pages of Euro-looking dudes until I found a style that didn't make me look like a pussy. All I wanted was a trim.

With a dull electric razor and sharp blade as his tools, the barber got to work. During the haircut, the argument I interrupted resumed in full force. I sat in the chair as the barber screamed in Arabic and aggressively scraped the back of my neck with his blade. After what seemed like the longest 15 minutes of my life, he finished. The cost was 20 guilders, and not a drop of blood was spilled. I walked out happy to be alive, and surprisingly pleased with the job.

Sporting my new outfit and with necklace in hand, I made my way to Lunch Room 52. Did I look like a bit of a douche? Perhaps. Did I look European? Absolutely. I arrived a few minutes early, and Emma was already waiting. I felt uncomfortable in my pleather pants, and it showed. In retrospect, I should have worn them in a bit.

Emma looked me up and down, and said bluntly, "Looks like someone went shopping."

"Yeah," I said, not sure if she was impressed or what.

"Hmm," she replied. "It's fine, I guess, but I wouldn't do it again."

"Got it," I said, making a note to retire the look. "Hungry?" I asked, eager to change subjects.

"No," she said.

"Really? You have to eat."

"Fine," she said reluctantly.

It was a rough start, but I figured things could only get better. Our destination was an Argentinean restaurant called Rancho near Dam Square. As we started the short walk, I once again felt like a teenager, this time on a date, not sure what to say and awkward as ever. All the usual questions seemed inappropriate, such as, "How's work?" or "Do anything fun today?" For the most part, we walked quietly down the street, getting used to each other. As we walked past the old church, I noticed a few cobblestones had been replaced by a bronze sculpture of a hand caressing a woman's breast.

"It's amazing where one can find beauty," I said, pointing at the artwork beneath our feet.

Emma looked at me like I was an idiot. "There's no beauty here," she said. "It's all crap."

Once at the canal, we made a right on Oudezijds Voorburgwal and passed one of the district's *pissoirs*. There are many great things America has borrowed from Europe. Thankfully, pissoirs are not one of them. Essentially, they are semi-enclosed structures invented by the French that allow for public urination without the expense of building a toilet. They're gross, but accepted as a necessary evil. Similar to bike theft, street pissing is an age-old problem in Amsterdam. For some thrill seekers, it's even a pastime. McDonald's and others made the problem worse by charging people to pee. In an attempt to contain the problem, the city installed public pissoirs throughout the city. Public they are, providing anyone walking by with the joy of hearing, smelling, and partially seeing men, and the occasional woman, urinate behind a metal barrier.

Reflections of red neon danced across the canal as we passed the streets hosting the prettiest women. It was between shifts, and all was quiet. Even Trompettersteeg was deserted. The district never completely sleeps however, and when the most attractive women are gone, the aesthetically challenged are busy at work, knocking on windows and displaying body parts in an attempt to win over a wandering john. Transition time is their time to shine.

A window marked Kamer 112 stood alone on Oudezijds Voorburgwal facing the canal. With a location next to the

Bulldog Café and around the corner from Trompettersteeg, it was valuable real estate. Yet inside, sitting on a stool in a thong with her legs spread open, was one of the most grotesque women I had ever seen. No taller than five feet, she must have weighed nearly 300 pounds, had thin balding hair, and a rash.

On top of it all, she was a gum chewer. In fact, every time I saw her, she was blowing bubbles, occasionally really big ones that would explode all over her face, to her delight. Whether or not she changed pieces between customers was anyone's guess. On busy nights, men would gather, daring each other to take turns. As a result, it was rumored she was a top earner. She sat patiently in her window as Emma and I passed. Just as I sneaked a glance, as if on cue, she winked and flashed a nipple.

After seeing her a few times, I affectionately gave her the nickname The Bubbler. It seemed appropriate. I started giving nicknames to other girls as well. I didn't do it intentionally. Names just popped into my head. They personalized my experience, and helped me keep track of everyone. The stunning girl in the La Vie en Rose doing crossword puzzles was The Puzzler. The girl from the welcoming committee clawing at her window was The Scratcher. Then there was The Baller, but we'll get into that later. Emma, though, was always just Emma.

We said little as we walked along the canal, but my mind was racing. I was beginning to think meeting her was a bad idea. Not only did she seem to have nothing to say, but for the first time I began worrying about my safety. If she had a pimp, or a boyfriend, he wouldn't be happy. Emma was meeting me off the clock. She was breaking the rules.

Our silence was punctuated by the sounds of bike horns and Algerian men whispering, "Hash, coca, ecstasy, Viagra, really good prices, you want, you want?" Then, just as we arrived at the restaurant, a man wearing a T-shirt reading, "Uranus . . . The truth is up there . . . Somewhere," stumbled by. Sexual references in Amsterdam were everywhere, and came at us from every possible direction.

It was a short but colorful walk, and I felt relieved as we sat down in a corner booth by the window. We looked at each other in silence for a few seconds, waiting to see who would speak first.

Finally, I said, "What's new?"

"I'm planning a trip to Tunisia," she said, forcing an uneasy smile. "I have to get out of this place."

A waiter came and took our order. I chose the steak fillet with sautéed vegetables. Emma ordered a chicken breast, baked potato, and vegetable salad. As we were in a steak restaurant, I asked why she didn't order one.

"I hate red meat," she said. "Too bloody."

Trying to lighten the mood, I said, "You can always ask them to cook it."

Emma just looked at me. No smile. Not even a grin.

During dinner, I finished two glasses of wine. Emma didn't have a sip. She had to work until three and had a long night ahead of her. Wine made her sleepy. Once the food arrived, the conversation softened. Like on a first date, we jumped from topic to topic. Cautiously, Emma told me a bit about herself. She was guarded and didn't share much. She seemed to care only about money.

"Money makes the world go around," she declared.

"Yeah, but money isn't everything. How about love?"

"What's that?" she laughed.

"It's just the most powerful thing," I said, not knowing what to say. For, truly, what is love? It's a word, but can it be defined? Is language capable of doing so? The ancient Greeks had seven words for it. We have one. We talk about love as though it's this singular thing, when really it means something different to each and every one of us, and between any two people, is constantly changing. The one thing I knew was that it's possible to have many loves in a lifetime. They come when you least expect. Some are platonic. Some are sexual. Some are divine. Some are a combination thereof. While all different, all are sacred, and can change you forever.

"Here's a question," I said. "If you had the choice of making $250,000 a year and being lonely, or $100,000 a year and being in love, which would you choose?"

"Stupid question," she responded. "I'd take the money."

As the conversation progressed, I learned more about her. She was born and raised in Holland and a hundred percent Dutch. She had never been to America, but wanted to visit. She had traveled to Canada, England, and Tunisia. She thought the Canadians were pussies, and the British pricks, but the Tunisians were all right. She hated cats, never finished high school, and didn't play any instruments.

During dinner Emma rarely talked about work. I didn't push it. In fact, I didn't want to touch the subject. Not yet.

Not until we built up some trust. The topic came up when she said she just made 1,000 guilders off a guy who only wanted to talk. She looked at me, making sure the compliment didn't pass me by, and asked, "So what's this book thing about again?"

"With your help, I want to write a book that captures the essence of the district," I said.

Emma seemed confused, and a bit sad.

"How can I help? I'm just a prostitute. I never finished high school, remember?"

"That doesn't matter," I replied. "You're smart. All I need is for you to be honest."

Emma gazed out the window in silence. I could tell she was uneasy. Looking back, I think her apprehension wasn't because of the subject, or need for honesty, but because she felt she had nothing to offer. Emma went on to tell me about her dreams of having money, becoming a mother, and moving to America.

I listened quietly, not saying much. Across from me sat one of the prettiest women I had ever seen. I could tell that, despite everything, she was a good person. Somehow, her life had gone horribly wrong. At times during dinner, I wanted to do nothing more than steal her away. I wanted to save her from the horror. Yet, never once during dinner, or our relationship, did I ever encourage her to leave. Nor did I ever pass judgment.

I remembered the conversation I overheard in Lunch Room 52 when the girls were talking about the men who wanted to save them. Early on, I made the decision that if Emma wanted to be saved, she would have to do it herself. She would have to come to her own conclusions. But, maybe, I could help. Maybe, I could nudge her in the right direction.

Emma continued to talk as we finished our meal. With every bite, she grew warmer. She explained one of her favorite things was to give gifts, and she had no money because of it.

Seizing the moment, I said, "I also like giving gifts," and pulled out the necklace.

Emma turned her eyes away in embarrassment. When I leaned across the table to give it to her, she pulled back. I had fucked up. The roses were fine, but I had gone too far with the necklace. It was too much. It was too personal. I should have known better. Emma just looked at me. I just sat there, convinced I had wrecked everything.

"Well," she said, "aren't you going to put it on?"

Emma inched out of the booth and came around to my side of the table. She slid in next to me and flipped her hair behind her head. Tilting her head back, she froze like a statue and didn't move until I had secured the necklace. The length of the chain forced me to press up against her as I unlocked the clasp and adorned her with silver.

The urge to kiss her was tempered by my knowledge of her profession, which in turn fueled my desire. I was in a place I had never imagined, with a woman who was forbidden. At the time, whether I was falling for her, or the idea of what she represented, was unclear.

When the waiter dropped off the check, Emma reached into her jacket and started flipping through a wad of cash. I pulled out my wallet and took care of it. It was the least I could do. Emma was appreciative. Before leaving the table, she wrote down her name and cell number on a napkin.

"Here's my cell in case you need me right away," she said. "I'm hard to reach at home."

I looked at the napkin and slid it into my pocket. "Emma's your real name?" I asked, assuming many in her profession used pseudonyms.

"Yeah," she said, "I felt safe telling you."

We left the restaurant and walked down Oudezijds Voorburgwal in the direction of the old church. By now the district was bustling, and the women were out in full force. I walked Emma down Trompettersteeg to her window.

Before entering, she said, "Thanks for dinner, and thanks again for the roses. No one has ever bought me flowers before. You're the first."

"I'll see you soon?" I asked.

"Yeah. Sure." Before she could finish, a tall German reeking of booze pushed me out of the way.

"Your turn's over. She's mine now," he snarled.

As Emma led the man in, I couldn't help but notice how beautiful the necklace looked against her soft neck.

Chapter 11

ON WEDNESDAY AFTERNOON I pedaled to Lunch Room 52 and ordered a meatball sandwich. Truth be told, it's difficult finding a decent place to grab lunch in Holland. It's almost as if the meal doesn't exist. Most Dutch go home or grab a sandwich from a vending machine. Eating out for lunch is not part of their spendthrift culture, which more or less consists of having one hot meal a day. After sampling a few sandwiches to varying degrees of success, I started searching for options. There were few to be found. Unless I wanted falafel, fries, and mayo, or perhaps a raw herring, I was generally out of luck.

Just as fish and chips is supremely British, raw herring is quintessentially Dutch, and has been for 600 years. At Oliver's request, I tried it—once. He said it was a rite of passage, and there was a popular *haringhuis* a block away in Haarlemmerplein. I held the stinky fish by the tail, dipped it in onions and pickles, leaned back, and took a bite. It was a mistake, and one I would not repeat.

Of all places, Lunch Room 52 was an odd choice. Who wants to eat a hot meatball sandwich surrounded by hundreds of guys blowing loads? Circumstances were less than ideal. Putting that detail aside, the outdoor seating gave me the chance to observe life in the district during the day.

I arrived at noon and sat in the same chair I did when I met Emma weeks ago. The sandwich arrived in record time, and I took a bite. The price was right, and I was in no position to be picky. Having spent more money than I wanted on two necklaces, one of which was hanging around the neck of a prostitute and the other lying on the bottom of a canal, I needed to get back on budget.

Sitting in the church square, with the welcoming committee doing their thing in the background, I watched as cars dropped off prostitutes on their way to work. I recognized some of the women. I saw The Puzzler from La Vie en Rose, and The Bubbler. It was different seeing them in street clothes. They seemed vulnerable. In just minutes, they would be transformed. One by one, they were dropped off in front of the church like children being dropped off at school, or perhaps like horses being led around a paddock before a race. Somehow, there was pageantry to it all. Most of the drivers were North African men, likely pimps, talking on cell phones and flashing gold.

As I took in the moment, a huge man in a suit came running around the corner directly at me. He looked pissed. I put down my sandwich and braced for impact. I wasn't sure if he was crazy, on drugs, or what. Maybe he was Emma's pimp, upset about dinner. I had no idea. What I did know was that he was moving fast and I had no time to escape.

Thankfully, I wasn't the target. He was a security guard and fixated on a man in sweatpants and loafers who, for some reason, was soaking wet. Without saying a word, the guard picked the guy up by the neck, threw him on the ground, spit on his face, and started kicking the shit out of him. All this while I was inches away, sipping an espresso. At one point, the guy's head came so close to the tire of a moving car I thought he was finished. Somehow, he freed himself and took off down the street, limping and blasting profanities.

Amidst the chaos, I learned he had touched a girl inappropriately. This was his punishment, along with being doused with water. I could hear the music still playing from the guard's headphones as he nonchalantly walked back to his post. Just another day's work. He didn't miss a beat.

The guy in sweatpants was just one of many men visiting the district that afternoon. As always, the place attracted an eclectic crowd. Businessmen and junkies wandered the streets, along with students and pensioners, all looking for a woman worthy of their 50 guilders. I even saw a father taking his son, possibly for his first sexual experience. This was apparently a tradition for some Dutch families, something you had to see to believe.

Several weeks into my explorations, I began recognizing several wandering johns, and they began recognizing me. At most, I would acknowledge them with a nod, as if to say, "Good seeing you again," or "Hope you're having a nice day." They initiated contact, to which I responded. It was the polite thing to do. In their mind, I had become part of their community, a member of their secret society.

Usually, a simple nod would be the extent of it. It didn't always work out that way. That afternoon, while fumbling to unlock the Purple Rocket from its chains, a guy started conversation. He was a middle-aged American, thin and balding with a Hapsburg jaw and intense acne around his neck and ears. As he stood over me, jewels of sweat formed on his forehead and inched down his face, only to be absorbed by the filthy collar of his blue Lacoste shirt. He was a clammy chap and made me nervous.

"So, what do you think of that brunette on Bethlemsteeg?" he asked.

"Huh?" I said.

"That cat I saw you walking with a few days ago."

"Oh, she's OK," I said dispassionately, alarmed he was talking about Emma.

"Well, man, I'm not sure. Last night, it was weird what I did. I figured the price for girls here is so cheap I would go trolling. I would stick my little penis in, and if I didn't like her, I would zip up, wash up, and go to another. I wouldn't even cum. I didn't even care. If I didn't like her pussy, I would just keep going until I found the perfect fit.

"First, I went for this blonde, thinking she was a good one. I dropped my pants and was ready to stick my little penis in. Then, just as I climbed on top, I looked up and saw a dog—a fucking bulldog. It was growling. No shit. I was thinking, put that fucker in a cage. Forget it. I zipped up and was out of there.

"My worst experience was with that brunette I saw you with," he continued. "She wanted to charge twenty-five extra to play with her tits. Stuff like that. It was bullshit, but taught me something. Now I say, if I want to play with your tits, will it be extra? You know what I mean. It gives me a little conversation. It's really good."

"Yeah man, thanks," I said, finally freeing my bike from its chains.

"Anytime," he said, as we parted ways.

Sex addiction is a serious problem in the district. This guy was an addict. I left without looking to see if Emma was around. I had enough for the day. I biked down Warmoesstraat, dodging junkies and tourists, and checked my messages once home. Emma called. She wanted to grab dinner. I was to meet her tomorrow at seven at our usual place, Lunch Room 52. I couldn't wait.

Chapter 12

I WOKE UP the next morning to a full day at university. A six-day weekend had come to an end. It was time to get back into it. Now deep in the semester, I had settled into a nice routine. Every Thursday morning, after a workout at Squash City, I would decide if I would bike or take the tram to school. While influenced by weather, the decision ultimately depended on how long I spent in the sauna. That morning I was running late, so opted for the tram.

My schedule began with comparative legal culture, followed by international dispute settlement, international social law, and comparative criminology. It was nothing short of a marathon. In criminology, the topic of the day was Holland's approach to cannabis.

To our surprise, we learned cannabis wasn't legal in Holland. Technically, it was a controlled substance. Possession and cultivation were misdemeanors, punishable by fines, and coffeeshops were illegal. Notwithstanding the law, the Ministry of Justice applied a tolerance policy, or *gedoogbeleid*, with respect to weed. Possession of five grams or less for personal use wasn't prosecuted, nor was the cultivation of up to five plants. This resulted in de facto decriminalization. While most Dutch believed people shouldn't go to jail for the plant, the subject remained controversial.

During class, any time the concept of justice came up, a Russian lawyer sitting next to German Kyle chuckled. Sometimes, he burst out laughing. After a while, it became disruptive. At first, I assumed Kyle was fucking with him under the table. That wasn't it.

Eventually, our professor asked, "Is there anything you'd like to share?"

Looking around, the Russian tentatively responded, "Are you serious? Justice and fairness, do such things exist? In Russia, justice is simply whoever is willing to pay the judge the most. That is all. That is law."

I thought he was kidding. He wasn't. Sure, our legal system in America is imperfect. There is corruption and unfairness. But at least we have a system. In Russia, corruption appeared to be the system—power and money the only things that mattered.

His comments led me to reflect on how sheltered most Americans are from the harsh realities of life. We are so quick to get caught up talking about, and obsessing over, lofty principles when, for much of the world, such concepts are little more than fairy tales. Life simply takes over. The concept of justice to a Russian lawyer seemed as foreign as the concept of love to a Dutch prostitute.

By five o'clock, class had come to an end. Having survived a long day in academia, it was time to dive back into the underworld. It was time to meet Emma. I took the No. 5 tram from university and transferred at Museumplein. Still carrying my backpack, I arrived in the district an hour early.

Given that lunch consisted of a vending machine sandwich, I was hungry as hell. I walked down Warmoesstraat, avoiding an elderly Yorkie dropping turds, and looked for a new place to grab a snack before dinner. I had already spent enough time at Lunch Room 52 and needed a change of scene, and a little tranquility.

I took a left on Oudebrugsteeg toward The Grasshopper and sat down at the counter of a kebab shop. Kebab shops were everywhere in Holland, like Starbucks in America. The place was deserted when I arrived except for a man behind the counter in a dirty tank top. He was so busy talking on his phone he didn't even acknowledge my presence.

With Middle Eastern music playing in the background, I sat at the counter until the call ended. I then ordered a falafel with traditional garlic sauce called *knoflooksaus*, a side of fries, and mayo. Before moving to Amsterdam, if someone would have told me I would be dipping fries into mayo once, sometimes twice, a day, I would have laughed. So be it. I was well on my way to becoming European.

While eating the falafel, the knoflooksaus started dripping down my arm. Since I was only given one napkin, I grabbed another. *No problem*, I thought. I thought wrong. When the man saw me reach for another, he started screaming.

"No more napkins! No more napkins!"

"Huh?" I asked. "I have a problem here."

"No more napkins. If you want, you pay!"

Then I got it. I understood why splitting the bill on a date is called going Dutch, and why a cast-iron pot over coals is called a Dutch oven. The Dutch are cheap, excessively so. Their thriftiness is habitual and part of their culture, left over from wartime. It's something in which they take pride. Their cheapness has even been studied, a report concluding the Dutch spend less than any other European country on holiday gifts.

German Kyle, well aware of this, had a list of jokes he repeated any chance he could, such as, "What's the thinnest book in the world? A Dutch gift catalogue!" Or, "What do Dutch kids get for Christmas? Coupons!" And his favorite, "Why are there no wishing wells in Holland? Too many people complained they got ripped off and wanted their money back!" Needless to say, the Dutch had their share of jokes about the Germans too.

Without question, much of Dutch stinginess is associated with food. They serve the smallest beer in Europe, and a Dutch sandwich generally consists of nothing more than a small piece of ham, a thin slice of cheese, and butter. While the Dutch might be generous when it comes to giving to charity, or helping those in need, don't even think about asking for an extra napkin, or an additional complimentary cookie. While the falafel man didn't appear Dutch, he had apparently assimilated.

With the knoflooksaus sliding down my arm at an alarming pace and about to make contact with my shirt, I needed to take action. Despite the warning, I grabbed another napkin and soaked up the sauce.

"You pay! You pay! Two guilders!" he yelled, reeking of sweat and curry.

"Two guilders! Are you kidding? No fucking way," I responded, turning away.

Then the unbelievable happened. He reached under the counter and pulled out a knife. Holding it above his head, he lurched forward.

"You pay, or I make you pay!" he screamed. "Fucking American. You fucking American, you pay!" he continued, waving the knife like a madman.

Holy shit, I thought. *This town is dangerous!* Terrified, I threw down some change and took off down the street, looking back to make sure I wasn't followed. Rattled by the encounter and in need of a drink, I wandered into Stone's Café on Warmoesstraat and ordered a Heineken.

Sitting at the bar, I watched as one guy after another stumbled in. The place was packed. Most of the men wore pleather, and had mustaches. While there was no sign indicating I was in a gay bar, there were clues. There was a gay cinema across the street, there were no women anywhere, and two dudes with exposed butt-cheeks were making out in a corner. That said, I just ordered my beer and was going to finish it. Then I'd move on.

As I sipped my drink, I had the feeling of being watched. Not surprising for a gay bar, but that wasn't it. Then, out of the corner of my eye, I saw the same dude who was checking me out the first time I sat with Emma. The nihilist was back. Just like before, he wore an overcoat and open-toe sandals. Just like before, he seemed to take an interest in me. What was his deal? Was he gay? Was he connected to Emma? Did he believe in nothing? I had no answers to any of these questions.

After a long stare in my direction, the man stood up from the bar and made his way to a pool table. His sandals made a distinctive flip flopping sound, like whips snapping. I avoided eye contact with him as two women entered the bar and sat beside me.

"Hey there, ladies," I said, with no purpose but to affirm my heterosexuality. I couldn't place it, but they seemed familiar.

"Oh, my God! You're American? We are too!" one of them exclaimed.

"Yeah," I said, "I'm American."

"That's an amazing coincidence," she continued.

"Not really," I replied, remembering how I knew them. They were the same two girls from Café Hill Street Blues, playing pool and screaming "ball in hole" after every shot. They had left a bad taste in my mouth. Not because they were lesbians, but because of their pool table etiquette.

"Anything going on tonight?" she asked.

"Just waiting to have dinner with a prostitute," I casually replied.

"What? Really?" she said coldly. "How much are you paying her?"

"Nothing. I'm writing a book with her."

"Sure you are," she said sarcastically.

"Yeah, we're friends. Why is that hard to believe?" I paused, and continued. "She's human, remember?"

At first she didn't say a thing. She only scowled in disgust, looking to her friend for support. Finally, she said, "You must really like her. I can tell by the look in your eyes. You're going to sleep with her."

"I'm not a customer," I said defensively.

"Yep," the other girl said, "he's going to sleep with her."

"What if I do?" I replied, annoyed.

"What do you mean? She's a whore!"

Testing the waters, I asked, "Even if we fall in love and no money changes hands?"

"She's a whore!" the girl continued.

"Well, what makes you so different from her? Don't you have a price?" I asked, as she flashed a glare of contempt. I continued, "Come on, if someone offered you a billion dollars to have sex with a stranger, any stranger, even a guy, you'd do it. In fact, most people would. Think of what you could do with a billion dollars."

"Perhaps," she conceded, reluctantly.

"How about a million dollars?" I continued.

"Perhaps," she mumbled.

"How about fifty thousand?" I continued.

"Maybe."

"How about ten thousand?" I pushed.

"I get your point," she conceded.

"We all have a price. For these girls, their price might just be a bit lower than yours." The women seemed to get it. I continued, "When we talk about prostitution, we're not talking about principle. It's not a question of ethics or morality, of right or wrong. It's a question of price. Sure, you might be worth more than fifty guilders, but how much more? Some of us, in our minds, are just more expensive than others. Perhaps this is why some women, like you, are so quick to condemn the women who work here. You just think you're worth more."

I finished my drink and left. It was time to see Emma. On my way out, I could hear them whispering, "He's definitely going to sleep with her." The fact they perceived Emma as untouchable disturbed me. Could she really be past redemption? I wondered about Emma's childhood, and how she could think she was worth 50 guilders.

As I walked down Warmoesstraat, I stopped on the corner of Enge Kerksteeg, a small street that leads to the Oude Kerk. For the first time, I noticed a flower shop full of cacti and tulips. I walked in with no intention but to surround myself with life.

Despite prostitution having been in Amsterdam for centuries, that didn't mean the Dutch accepted it any more than my two American friends. Even in Holland, it's not just some other job. There's a powerful stigma that attaches, and sticks, to anyone in the business. Many Americans think the Dutch are an ultra-liberal people who don't place moral judgment on prostitution and drugs. They do, but generally refrain from telling others how to live. In America, it can be argued we do the opposite. We are quick to tell everyone how to live, while making excuses for ourselves.

Emma was waiting when I arrived, pacing back and forth.

"I'm sorry, I have to work tonight," she said. "Today's been shit. I only made two hundred guilders. I'm flying to Tunisia soon. I need to make at least two hundred more."

I just looked at her.

"Listen," she said, "meet me here tomorrow, same time. I'll be all yours." I couldn't think of anything to say. All I could think of was her standing in her window all night long. "Please don't be angry," she continued.

"Emma," I said, trying to save the night, "let me loan you the money. It's only two hundred guilders. You need the night off. Let's have a nice dinner. You can pay me back later."

"No," Emma said, surprisingly. "That's your money."

"Emma, I'm not giving it to you. It's a loan," I said, making sure not to break my code.

She seemed unable to distinguish the difference, as if in her world there was none. "No, and never ask me again," she repeated.

"I don't want you to work tonight," I pleaded, fearing this might be our last chance to connect.

"I'm serious," she said. "If you ever offer me money again, that will be the last you see of me." I went to hold her hand. She pushed me off.

"I can be a bitch," she whispered. "Tomorrow, I'm yours," she said indifferently, as she turned around and made her way to her window. It was time for her next shift.

Chapter 13

AFTER EMMA WENT back to work, I didn't know what to do. I had no plans. While exhausted from my day at university, I didn't want to go back to my apartment. I didn't want to hang with friends. I didn't want to think about much of anything, but I had no choice. Emma was on my mind. I wondered how many men she would be with that night, and how not one of them would have any idea who she was. Worse yet, I hoped she was busy. At least then, maybe, she would be happy. I would later learn that, on an average night, Emma could have anywhere from five to 15 customers. Men would pass by, look her up and down, and make an off-the-cuff decision whether or not they wanted to fuck her. Many wouldn't even ask her name. For 15 minutes, she would be stripped of her humanity, over and over again.

As I wandered through the red lights, I reflected on my progress with the book. My round-trip ticket had been purchased. I was set to leave Holland in December. It was October. Despite my connection with Emma, I had doubts whether she was willing, or able, to open up. I had every reason to believe she would keep leading me on, perhaps until I became a customer. Given my feelings, I started questioning my resolve. What would happen if I was really tested? What would it take for me to cross the line? One of the reasons I refused to become a customer was that I wanted to build trust with Emma. I started to doubt whether trust was something that even existed in the district.

In need of a bathroom, I stumbled into the Bulldog coffeeshop on Oudezijds Voorburgwal. The street name reminded me of yet another of German Kyle's favorite jokes. "What's the best thing about marrying a Dutchman?" he would ask. "On your wedding day they give you something long and hard . . . their last name!" *So true*, I thought, and let out a chuckle. Despite having lived in Holland for some time now, the language was still killing me.

There are several Bulldog coffeeshops in Amsterdam. Not only was this location the oldest, it was the oldest coffeeshop in the city. Founded in 1974, it started off as a room in a former sex shop where friends would gather to smoke weed. Tourists soon caught on, and that was that. The modern coffeeshop was born. After wading through plumes of smoke and decades of history, I arrived at the bathroom. The door was locked. I sat down and waited.

The coffeeshop was filled with American and British tourists. It was the usual scene—mellow vibes, quiet conversations, slow movements, and lots of smoke. I watched as some Brits unraveled cigarettes and scattered weed on piles of tobacco. Ten minutes passed, and the door remained locked. I had to go bad, but was not about to use the pissoir.

No chance. One of the Brits saw I was alone and invited me to join his group. With Y2K months away, they were sharing plans for the millennium.

"I'm going to a party outside Rome," one of them said. "There will be thousands of people, dressed in togas, celebrating like it was two thousand years ago. I hear they're going to have sheep," he said with a grin. "You all should come."

"I can't," another said. "I'm going to Stonehenge. I'm pretty sure we'll have sheep too."

Amidst all this sheep talk, I continued watching the door. There was no movement whatsoever. It had now been 15 minutes. Growing impatient, I wandered over and listened for signs of life. Something was going on inside.

Now, I am not a knocker. I am all about letting people pee in peace, and otherwise conduct their business. I had no desire to wage a bathroom door war, but there are lines that must be drawn, and limits to anyone's patience. At that moment, lines were being crossed. It sounded like someone was using the Bulldog as a boudoir.

It started with a light knock. The moaning only got louder. I then heard laughter. I knocked again and rattled the doorknob, making sure my presence was known. I even yelled *doei*, meaning "goodbye" in Dutch, hoping they would get the hint. The bathroom was clearly not being used for legitimate purposes.

After what seemed like an eternity, the door opened and out poured the American girls from Stone's Café, kissing and holding hands, their pants unbuttoned. First I saw them at Café Hill Street Blues, then at Stone's, and now here.

Our lives were intertwined. *Oh, my fucking God*, I thought. Seeing them the third time was definitely the charm.

"It's all yours," one of them said, toilet paper trailing from her shoe. I took care of business, nodded goodbye to the Brits, and returned to the streets. I didn't want to roam the district that night. It made me feel like I was back at square one. But I knew I couldn't count on Emma. If the book was going to happen, I would need to make additional contacts, or at least try. I needed to put myself back in the current.

I passed Kamer 112, which had its curtain drawn, and walked down Trompettersteeg. The street was crowded, and it started to rain. I had an umbrella but didn't use it. The crowds made that impracticable, and the rain felt good as it sprinkled down upon me.

Looking around, I saw many of the usual girls. Several had already rejected my book proposal. They looked down as I passed. A few rolled their eyes, knowing I was just some kid trying to write a book. To them, life in the district was not some social issue to address. It was about money, plain and simple. Give it to them, or get the fuck out.

As I walked through the De Wallen, surrounded by hostility on all sides, I made eye contact with a young woman I hadn't seen before. She looked Scandinavian, and stood in a room decorated with a box of Kleenex and jar of lubricating jelly. She paced anxiously behind her window. Unlike the other women, she wore a floral dress that hung below her knees. As I looked at her, lost in the sadness of the moment, I heard knocking behind me. At first I didn't react, hoping it would stop. It got louder.

As I turned to check it out, a group of missionaries paraded by, pushing me up against the window behind me. I made impact with the glass, only to find myself face to face with one of the most ghoulish women in the district—even more menacing than The Bubbler. She was sweating profusely as if she had a fever.

Looking deep into my eyes, she opened her window and said in a thick Eastern European accent, "Fitty guilda, and you can leek da puzie."

She then started licking her lips and flashed a breast that looked like a deformed eggplant. In her mind, it was my lucky day. I turned around to find the Scandinavian girl laughing.

"Not your type, huh?" she said, calling me over.

"Not really. I'm not looking for action. I'm just doing some thinking."

"You're in the wrong place for that," she said, laughing innocently. "Believe it or not, this is my first night. Sure you don't want to come in?" she asked politely.

"Nah," I said.

Hesitating, she continued, "Would you change your mind if I told you it was also my birthday?" *No way*, I thought. Her first day working, and her birthday, too? She had to be playing me. If she wasn't, I could think of nothing worse. Either way, I was going to pass.

"Well, come by and visit sometime. My name's Michelle," she said, closing the door.

Eager to get out of the rain and ready to leave the district, I walked down Warmoesstraat and stumbled into Café

Hill Street Blues. It had been a while since I was there with Oliver, and much had happened. I smiled at the cardboard cutout of Uncle Sam, passed the graffiti wall, and sat by myself downstairs. Sipping a Heineken and smoking a joint of Jack, I looked out at the canal for an hour as bongo drums echoed off the fifteenth-century buildings.

Before leaving, I made my way to the graffiti wall and grabbed a pen. I had been in Amsterdam for almost two months. It was time to leave my mark. A quote from Albert Einstein came to mind. In red letters, I wrote, "Life is like riding a bicycle. To keep your balance, you must keep moving."

It was raining and cold when I headed out. Ironically, I had left my bike at home. I opened my umbrella for the first time that night and began the long walk back, hoping to see Emma tomorrow, but not holding my breath.

Chapter 14

EMMA WAS STANDING near the old church when I arrived. She wasn't a minute late. *So far, so good*, I thought, as the bells sounded. The next few hours would give us time for dinner and to start working on the book. As I approached, she stood and gazed into the distance. She didn't need to say anything for me to know what was going on.

"I have to work again tonight," she said coldly. "I need the money."

I just looked at her in silence. I couldn't believe it.

"Don't look at me like that," she said adoringly. "We can still eat. Where are we going?"

We walked in the direction of the central station, stopping in front of Malaysian, Portuguese, and Thai restaurants. None of them were to her liking.

"Too much fish," she grumbled. "How about the place we went last time?"

"Sounds good," I said, as we walked back in the direction of Dam Square.

When we arrived, the restaurant was full and had a 30-minute wait. Thankfully, the hostess remembered us and found a table upstairs. It soon became clear why the table was empty. We weren't so lucky after all.

Located next to the kitchen, the temperature must have been at least 10 degrees hotter than the rest of the restaurant. Moments after sitting down, I began sweating. It was like dining in a sauna. I stripped down to my T-shirt, leaving a pile of clothes to my side. Emma didn't take off anything, and remained wrapped in her knee-length leather coat.

"Aren't you a bit hot?" I asked.

"God, you're a smart one," she replied. "How'd you figure that out?"

"Just a guess," I replied.

"Well, I wasn't planning on going out," she said. "When I saw you, I changed my mind."

"What does that have to do with not taking off your coat?" I asked.

"As I said, I wasn't planning on leaving my window for long," Emma said. "The coat is just about all I have on."

Basically, Emma had come to dinner in the nude. By most standards, not a bad second date. The thought of her naked body under her coat was alluring, but it saddened me as well. As between the two emotions, the sadness won out. It wasn't even close.

After an awkward silence, the waiter arrived. We didn't bother looking at the menu. Dinner would be the same as before, except this time I ordered a side of baked tomatoes. I had to change it up a little. Emma didn't change a thing.

Given the blazing heat and loud music, our conversation moved at a slow pace. Emma was anything but talkative. She already had a long day, and it was just beginning. I didn't press her with questions. The last thing she needed was an interrogation. Rather, we quietly ate and enjoyed each other's company like a couple who'd been together for years. After the meal, she asked if I minded if she smoked a cigarette. I didn't stand in the way of her deadly habit.

"I always need to keep busy," she said. "That's the only reason I smoke. I hate waiting around."

"How do you stand in a window then?" I asked.

"I smoke a lot. Until the first customer comes, I almost go insane. I can't take this shit much longer. Men are shit, but some are OK. You are OK, and this one guy, this regular, is helping me out. He wants to buy a restaurant in Utrecht. I'll be the manager."

"Would you be happy with a job like that?" I asked.

"Are you kidding?" Emma said, surprised by the question. "I could be a normal person again. That's what I want, more than anything."

"What do you mean? You are normal."

Blushing, and ashamed, she said quietly, "David, I'm a prostitute." Emma seemed to know something I didn't understand at the time, or at least didn't want to accept.

"No, Emma, you're more than that," I said, "and I need you for the book. When can we start?"

"Oh, I don't know," she said tentatively. "I'm real busy for the next month. I have to wallpaper my home, go to a birthday party, and some other stuff. I'll help, but later," she said indifferently. I could tell she was afraid. By asking her to open up, I was asking her to be vulnerable.

"Maybe I could help you wallpaper," I said.

"Never," Emma said sharply. "I can never have someone from this world come to my home. That's forbidden. Sorry, you've seen me in a window. When I come to Amsterdam, I leave myself behind. If I were to take you home, my worlds would collide. You know what else?" she said. "My worst nightmare is coming home and having a guy there. Great life, huh? Still want to interview me?"

"Emma, please, I'm your friend."

"Yeah, sure. Then why'd you give me this?" she asked, opening her coat and exposing the necklace between her breasts.

Before I had a chance to respond, the waiter came with the check. Emma grabbed it. "Eighty-four guilders. My treat," she said.

I tried to pay, but she would have none of it. I was flattered, but it seemed wrong. Now she would have to make the money back. Maybe a fuck would do it, or perhaps two blowjobs. Either way, while touched by her generosity, I felt guilty. The last thing I wanted was to cause her to spend more time in her window. Now, I had unwittingly done just that.

As we walked back into the district, I reached to hold her hand. Like before, it was automatic, a natural thing to do. This time, she didn't let go. My heart started racing.

"Look, David," she said. "I need to see if I have a window for the night. If none are available, I'll stay with you. Follow me for a few minutes."

Taking my hand, Emma led me down Oudezijds Achterburgwal. As we walked side by side, I wasn't ready to say good night. More than anything, I wanted to spend the night with her, roaming the city, sharing memories, and escaping the confines of our lives. I wanted to sit in a café along the banks of a canal and stare into her eyes, so we both could remember how sacred life is and how nothing else matters. The night was going too well for it to end so soon.

Beautiful women drenched in red swayed on both sides of the canal which reflected the light like an impressionist painting. Despite the beauty all around us, Emma looked at the prostitutes with disgust. There seemed to be little community between them. What existed was mostly contempt. Halfway to our destination, we passed a marble penis spouting water into the air. This was the marble penis of the Casa Rosso, one of Amsterdam's famous sex shows. It was a busy night, and a line formed outside.

Sex shows were everywhere in the district, like theaters on Broadway, and competition for the tourist dollar was fierce. Accordingly, shows tried to be as creative as possible. One advertised a girl who would thrust a lit candle inside her and drip hot wax over her body. Another promised a girl who could smoke a cigar from her vagina, blowing smoke rings into the crowd.

In all the shows, audience participation was key. Once on stage, volunteers could be asked to eat a banana from a girl's vagina, or lie down with their shirt off only to have a girl stick a magic marker inside her, squat down, and write the words "I Love U" on their chest. With the price of entry ranging from 50 to 75 guilders, there was money to be made, and aggressive doormen did their best to usher in as many tourists as possible. For many, the Casa Rosso is what they think of when they remember the district, and perhaps Amsterdam itself.

While I didn't frequent these shows, I had stumbled into one during my first trip to Amsterdam years ago. I remembered the night well. With the crowd going crazy from the magic marker act, a guy and two girls came on stage. The women, a blonde and a brunette, were in their twenties. The guy was around 60. They got naked, engaged in foreplay, and began looking for a volunteer.

They found an American in the front row. He was sitting with friends. To the cheers of the crowd, he stepped on stage. The girls rubbed up and down against him as the cheers grew louder. Everyone thought this was as far as the act would go. All of a sudden, the brunette undid his belt and whoosh, pulled his pants down to his ankles. She then asked him if he was shy, to which he politely replied, "No, ma'am."

"Good," she said, and whoosh, grabbed his underwear and pulled them down. To his credit, the American just laughed, his junk hanging out for all to see. His friends began chanting his name. "Johnny, Johnny, Johnny." Then, just as he was getting ready to pull up his pants, the blonde pulled out a florescent condom. She held it up to the audience. The crowd roared, and the chanting grew louder.

Johnny stood frozen on stage. With the help of the other girl, they unrolled the condom, slid it on, and began giving him head. The audience went nuts as the American did his best to maintain balance, his eyes rolling to the back of his head. Then, as if the show hadn't gone far enough, the old man traded places with the brunette and went to work.

At first, Johnny didn't notice. When he realized what was going on, it was too late. His knees wobbled and boom, he was finished. The crowd was on its feet, giving Johnny the ovation of a lifetime. In the spirit of Amsterdam, he took a bow and returned to his seat.

Emma and I squeezed through the crowds and continued on our way. As we walked down the street, passing rows of women, we came across a young boy sitting alone in front of a window. He must have been no older than seven. His parents were nowhere to be found. I had seen kids in the district before, but always with family. I had never seen anything like this.

I mentioned it to Emma and she shook her head.

"This is no place for a kid," she said. Making sure he wasn't lost, Emma approached the boy. She asked if he was OK, and if his mother knew where he was. He nodded, and pointed to a woman standing in her underwear. His mom was there after all. Working. When the woman saw us, she opened her window and scolded us for talking to her son, and more importantly, blocking her window.

"Typical shit," Emma said in disgust. The scene upset her, which was surprising. I would have thought she wouldn't have cared.

When we arrived on the corner of Molensteeg and Oudezijds Achterburgwal, Emma told me to grab a drink in the Old Sailor while she talked to the landlord.

"Only girls are allowed upstairs," she said, with a touch of exclusivity. Emma rang a buzzer next to a window-less green door and disappeared up a narrow stairway. The sounds of a European soccer match filled the air as I leaned on the statute of the old sailor and waited for her to return.

She came back a few minutes later, expressionless. "I have a window until three. I'd better get to work," Emma said, looking at the ground. Our night together was over.

Before turning to walk away, she gave me a hug. I wanted to say everything was going to be OK, but I couldn't. It wasn't. I felt the warmth of her body against mine as I held her close, wishing things were different.

"Call me if you need help wallpapering," I said.

"I'll be fine. You've already helped me enough," she said, as she walked off alone in the direction of the old church, and I ordered another beer.

Chapter 15

IT WAS ALMOST 10 o'clock when I finished my second pint of Heineken. A group of men in orange shirts had gathered to watch a soccer match. With the television suspended from the ceiling, they stood in a huddled mass with their heads tilted back, as if praying to some divinity. I watched the last few minutes of the game, which, in all it's glory, ended in a scoreless tie. With the men hailing it as one of the best games ever, I grabbed another beer and stared out the window at the women across the canal.

Going into the evening, I already had serious doubts whether Emma would be willing to help. The events of the night had only made things worse. Once again, she had brought me close, only to push me away. I began thinking this was how she treated all her men. I was just one of them.

When you are young and naive, like I was, you think love, purpose, destiny, and other such things matter to everyone. You get older, and realize for many, the only thing that matters is money, their only value system being whether they are putting money in their pocket, or not. While I was lost deconstructing the philosophical and metaphysical meaning of our relationship, Emma was lost thinking how many guys she needed to fuck to make the next thousand guilders. The dichotomy was stark, depressing, and increasingly self-apparent. She existed in a different realm. In her world, money was all that mattered. There was little room for anything else. Emma was intrigued by me, nothing more. All those thoughts and more spiraled through my head as I sipped my beer, alone.

That said, in my heart, I knew our connection was real. I knew it transcended the district, and I had seen shades of her generosity. A few minutes earlier, she paid for dinner, and then stopped to make sure the boy was OK. She didn't need to do that. It wasn't behavior I expected. She had proven herself wrong. Despite her protestations, money wasn't the only thing that mattered. There was more to Emma than she was willing to admit. She wasn't completely turned. Not yet. There was still a part of her left. Looking back, maybe that's what threatened her the most. I saw something in her she wanted to forget, or let go of. In any event, I knew I had to be patient, but it was difficult. My time was running out. The millennium was upon us.

As I got up to leave the bar, I once again had the feeling of being watched. A few seconds passed, and it didn't go away. I looked around. Sure enough, I saw a familiar face. It wasn't a good one. It was the mystery man I'd seen twice before—first at Lunch Room 52, then at Stone's Café. Now, he was here. As before, he wore an overcoat and open-toe sandals, and was as unnerving as ever. Who the hell was this guy? Was I being followed? Amsterdam is small, and things do happen in threes. After all, I'd run into those American girls three times now. Praying it was just a case of red light paranoia, I left the bar, hoping to never see him again.

The night was young, so I decided to roam the streets before retiring. A mellow walk along the canals was in order. Sluggish from drinking wine and beer, I walked into a convenience store to purchase two cans of Red Bull. One might have been enough, but I had grown a bit immune to the stuff. I offered a 50-guilder note for two drinks. The guy looked at me like I had given him $1,000 for a stick of gum. I flipped through some postcards while he reluctantly dug around for change, shaking his head.

"I don't have change for this," he said coldly.

"Really?" I said. "I gave you fifty guilders. That's only twenty-five dollars."

Scowling, he replied, "Hold on," and walked out of the shop. Customer service on the Continent was something else. People actually try hard not to sell things. This guy was a prime example. I stood alone for several minutes until he returned with change. I took my two Red Bulls, guzzling one, and hit the streets.

Walking down Oudezijds Achterburgwal, I made a left on Monnikenstraat and passed a row of seven windows. The women were all in their spots, looking for work. Six of them were Asian and wore lace lingerie; the other was dark-skinned and wore a satin corset. All were gorgeous, and had the same glazed-over look in their eyes. At such a young age, they had already become ghosts.

Making my first right, I found myself standing in a square off Gordijnensteeg. Four Middle Eastern men played hide-the-pea on a cardboard box and gestured for me to join. I respectfully declined and walked a few paces to Bloedstraat. The energy was different there. Somehow, it was more imposing.

Because of the current that flows through the district, most never stop moving for more than a few seconds, unless they have business to attend to, or there is something special to see. That night a crowd had gathered. I immediately saw what created the pileup.

In a window stood a girl more beautiful than any movie star or model. She was like an idealized painting or Greek goddess, and wore only a white bra and red thong. At least 15 men stood and stared as she danced in her window. The more they looked, the more they had to. I nicknamed her The Looker. Despite the crowds, she had no customers. The men bunched around her window reminded me of a group of penguins on an iceberg, waiting to see who would jump in the water first. Only then would they know there were no sharks around. I waited patiently for someone to test the waters. Five minutes passed. No one did.

Only one explanation made sense. Men don't visit prostitutes just for sex, but to live out fantasies. That I knew. Maybe The Looker was just too perfect. She was beyond imagination. She was too good. Rather than spend 15 minutes with perfection, men would rather visit less attractive women, ordinary women. Women they have actually fantasized about in real life. While The Looker was mesmerizing, that was all. She was out of their league, even for a prostitute.

There are many types of men who visit the district. While some fit into the group described, others simply want to fuck the hottest girl possible. Both were in the mix that night, and eventually two Americans mustered up the confidence to give it a go. With the crowd buzzing, they approached her window in matching Bulldog T-shirts and whispered something in her ear. Apparently, they both wanted to go in together. She pushed them away and slammed the door.

"Get the fuck out of here," The Looker hollered from behind her window.

Out of the blue, an old man with a cane stumbled by and made his way to her. He was likely 80, but looked 100. Hunched over and decrepit, I wasn't sure if he was going to make it. When he finally arrived, to a gasp from the crowd, The Looker opened her door and let him in, closing her curtain behind. The show was over, at least for another 15 minutes.

With The Looker conducting business, I drank my second can of Red Bull and moved on, but I didn't go far. My attention was drawn to the next window over. In it was a tiny blonde doing her best to look like Baby Spice from the Spice Girls. With the song "Wannabe" playing in the background, she worked her body into all kinds of positions as if auditioning for Cirque du Soleil. She became The Stretcher. I stood nearby as a man in a bomber jacket and green slacks approached.

"No toys, no licking, no touching, no kissing," The Stretcher announced. "Just fucking."

"Yum," the man replied.

"You in?" she asked, putting a leg behind her head like a ballerina.

"Oh, yeah," he replied, "but only if I can do it bareback."

She glared.

"You know, without a condom," he continued.

"You can fuck your sister without a condom," she yelled, slamming the door.

The district can be a hostile place. That night, the hostility was out in full force. Prostitutes in Amsterdam aren't paid to be nice. They're paid to have sex, and the women have no problem screaming at guys wasting their time, compromising their safety, or crossing the line. There is a system. There are rules. If a guy goes against the system, there are consequences.

The johns have rules too, known to those who frequent the place. They are safety tips, or best practices, and shed important light on the district. As there are no manuals passed around, or seminars offered, first timers often have to learn the hard way.

Let's start with Rule Number One. Before picking a girl and getting to business, always question her about the price and, specifically, what's included. Many, if not most, will charge extra for fondling, sex acts, positions, and even removing clothes. Sucking tits will cost you, and kissing is forbidden. Don't even ask. A 50-guilder experience can quickly become much more with all the extras. Remember, once in a room it's hard to negotiate. You lose your leverage. Reality shifts. So, negotiate from the outside, on neutral ground. Of all the rules I heard, this appeared to be the most important.

Rule Number Two came in a close second, and is related to the first. Never ask for a discount. Not in the windows. The word has no meaning. Fifty guilders is the cost of entry. Period. Other terms can be negotiated, but not the base rate. Simply asking for a discount can result in a door being slammed in your face, being yelled at, or worse. Fifty guilders is cheap to begin with. The girls know that. When someone asks for a discount, it's insulting to the core, and there's no saving the relationship. Asking for a discount is essentially pressing the self-destruct button. Sure, they'll still fuck you, but it likely won't be any good.

Rule Number Three, well, is just good dealmaking. Agree on when the clock starts ticking. It shouldn't start immediately, but after she undresses. You're paying for sex, not a strip tease. She can undress on her own time, and both of you should watch the clock. Not just her. Every second is key, and can make the difference between a successful effort and a failed one. Once in a room, it's easy to lose track of time, especially if you're stoned, drunk, or both. Some regulars will even ask women to give five-minute, one-minute, and 30-second warnings, just like when taking a standardized test. Remember, time flies. *Tempus fugit.*

Rule Number Four is really a warning to the wise. Avoid girls displaying outlandish and showy behavior, like flashing boobs, playing with their pussy, inserting toys, and engaging in other eye-catching activities. Most likely, they have a bad reputation, few repeat customers, and make their money preying on tourists. If you have a product, you have to advertise. Nothing's wrong with that. But if a girl looks like too much fun, watch out. Once inside, they are likely to change, become mean, or turn into a cold fish. There are exceptions, but beware.

On the other side of the coin, Rule Number Five is avoid girls who never smile and won't look you in the eye. She likely has no intention of pleasing you, and won't. If the girl is playing too hard to get, chances are she's not available. Sure, she'll lie there, and you can fuck her, but that's about it. No value added. Visiting a girl in Amsterdam can be robotic. It's not the girlfriend experience. For many, getting a blowjob is more like getting milked than having sex. It can be disconcerting, and clinical. Sex becomes a medical procedure. Solid eye contact can help change that, and make it more personal.

Rule Number Six, building on Rule Number Five, is build rapport. Mention something other than sex and money when negotiating, and see how she responds. Even small talk about the weather will do. Anything works. If she has any interest in pleasing you, she will engage, or at least try. Be wary of the girl who ignores you, is rude, or acts like you are taking up her time. There's a lot of anger in the district. Move on. Importantly, always look for a bucket or glass of water in a girl's room. Some are quick to drench any guy who pisses them off, and it's generally not a risk worth taking. Especially in cold winter months.

Rule Number Seven requires dedication, but the payoff can be worth it. Conduct a stakeout. If you see a girl who interests you, wait for another guy to enter, give it 15 minutes, and watch his reaction when he leaves. If he had a good experience, he might just tell you about it. If he had a bad one, he'll tell you for sure, hoping to deprive the girl of a customer. Needless to say, there are drawbacks with this approach. No one likes sloppy seconds, and the visuals can be disturbing. No doubt the Americans in Bulldog T-shirts were not waiting around for the 80-year-old to finish the job, and give it another try. Seeing the guy before can certainly affect your mojo, but the information can be priceless.

Rule Number Eight is just common sense. Don't try to stick a finger up a girl's ass. That is, without permission. In addition to being antisocial, and sneaky, it's been said doing so can result in the cost of your experience automatically tripling. Fifty guilders becomes 150, just like that. The move is called The Tripler, and should be avoided. Just good manners. Also, it might result in security being called. So, don't do it.

Rule Number Nine comes right out of sex ed class. Don't try to fuck a girl without a condom. You will get yelled at. Contrary to what some believe, a girl won't do anything for money, especially if it could kill them. Remember, they are human beings, and safety comes first.

Finally, Rule Number Ten is look for an Adam's apple. Things aren't always as they seem.

These rules are the unspoken Ten Commandments of the district, at least for those who know their way around.

With the Red Bull kicking in, I wandered north on Bloedstraat, passing several dimly lit windows perched above flights of stairs. A group of men congregated in front of one. A beautiful blonde stood motionless above. From street level, she was imposing. While probably only six feet tall, she looked like a giant. She was cloaked in blue light, unlike the usual red, and wore leather boots and black lingerie.

An American wearing a college sweatshirt walked up the stairs. He exchanged words with the woman and hurried back down. Upon flashing his friends a thumbs-up, one of them handed over 50 guilders and gave him a pat on the back. He walked back up and disappeared behind her curtain. For his buddies, the next 15 minutes would be a waiting game. I listened as they debated who would go next. They had found their girl.

"First time in Amsterdam?" I asked.

"Yeah. We're backpacking through. It's our junior year."

"Where are you staying?"

"Hotel Kabul," he replied. "Know it?"

"Yep," I replied. Not only did I know it, I had stayed there during my first trip to Amsterdam years ago. Located on Warmoesstraat, and prominently listed in *Let's Go Europe*, the hotel attracted lots of Americans. The place was a dump, but cheap and centrally located.

With nowhere to go, I chilled with the group as they waited for their friend. To our surprise, after a few minutes, he came running out, sweating, his belt undone.

"I'm going to kick that guy's ass. He's fucking dead."

"Who's dead? What are you talking about?" one of them asked.

"That fucking guy. He's fucking dead."

"What guy?" his friend asked again. We looked at the window and saw the prostitute standing outside, waving her fists. We couldn't figure out what was going on. Then I looked closer. The prostitute, glowing in the blue light, had an Adam's apple . . . and a penis. She grabbed the base of her cock and twirled it around like a lasso, letting out a bellowing laugh.

"Come get me big boy!" she said with a grin and deep voice. "I'm all yours."

Seizing the moment, one of the guys starting singing Aerosmith's "Dude Looks Like a Lady." The others joined in. One of them started harmonizing.

"It's not funny. Fuck off, all of you," he screamed, storming off along the canal. His friends followed, still singing. As they scurried off, one of them tripped on a cobblestone and went flying, coming dangerously close to a canal. Had he flown a few inches further, we would have had a swimmer.

Inadvertent swimming happens regularly in Amsterdam, and is not a good thing. In additional to the water being freezing, canals are filled with sewage from houseboats and a massive amount of debris. As many as 15,000 bikes are fished out every year, and pulling someone out can be challenging. As I watched the action, I continued keeping an eye on our friendly neighborhood transvestite.

"There's still time on the clock. Want a turn?" she graciously asked from across the street. By now, I had affectionately nicknamed her The Baller.

"Thanks, but I don't think you're my type," I replied.

"You never know until you try," The Baller said. "You know where to find me."

"I certainly do," I said, waving goodbye.

It was only later I learned Bloedstraat was famous for hosting the most beautiful transvestites in the district. So beautiful they could fool just about anyone. The blue lights were the clue something was different. We just thought it was cool mood lighting.

A junkie on a car clipped his toenails into a canal as I continued on my stroll. Soon, I found myself at the Oude Kerk. Like a magnet, it always seemed to draw me back. It had a center of gravity all its own. Just as I was getting ready to call it a night, I heard someone call my name. It was Michelle, the birthday girl.

"Good seeing you again," she said, wearing the same floral dress as before. "Sorry for my attitude the other night. I was having a bad day. My boyfriend threw me out on my birthday. This is the last place I want to be, but I have nowhere else to go. It's safer than the streets. The men have been horrible. One even wanted to fuck with the window open."

"I'm sorry," I said, realizing it might have been her birthday after all. "Happy belated birthday, I guess."

"Thanks," she replied. "Want to come in? That would make things better."

"You're beautiful," I said, "but I'm not here for that. I'm working on a book. Interested in helping?"

"I've only been working two days. I'm not sure I've much to say, but I'll help if I can. Come back in ten minutes. I'll give you my number. There are cameras everywhere. I have to be careful." I wondered what she had to be careful about, and promised to return. It had already been a hell of a night. Now, it would be at least 10 minutes longer.

I wasn't confident Michelle would be able, or willing, to help. But it was worth a shot, and one of my best opportunities yet. All doors, other than Emma's, had been slammed in my face. Just like when rafting down a river, at this point in my journey, I was simply trying to stay in the current, avoid the rocks and eddies, and see what was around the bend.

Still in the heart of the De Wallen, I walked down Goldbergersteeg and turned around at the end of the dead-end street. Over the centuries, so much had happened on these streets. So many moments had come and gone. Now, I was the only one standing there, completely anonymous. Anonymity is what the district sells. No questions are asked. No names are given. There is a freedom that results, which can be intoxicating. This is true for both men and women, and was likely one of the reasons no one wanted to help with my book. Just like the men, the women wished to remain invisible.

At that moment, alone on a dead-end street, I felt more anonymous than ever. Suddenly, a window opened inches from me. I expected to see a guy walk out. Instead, out came a beautiful girl. She wore only a tank top, booty shorts, and tall leather boots. I had never seen her before. Lost in my thoughts, I was caught off-guard, and froze. My defenses were down.

"Want to come inside America boy?" she said confidently.

"Nah," I said. "I'm not here for that. I'm working on a book."

"Ah, smart and good looking. Now you must come in!"

"No thanks," I said. "You're pretty, for sure, but I don't pay for sex. Sorry."

"That's OK," she said. "How about you come in and we just talk for a bit. I'm interested in your book. My name's Ava."

She opened her door and gestured for me to enter. Without giving it much thought, I did as I was told. Ava closed the curtain. Just like that, for the first time, I was behind a window.

The world seemed different from the inside. The noise from the street was muffled. The air was warm and heavy. There was a feeling of calm. The real world remained inches away, but I felt transported. My perception and understanding of things changed. When I looked at Ava, I no longer saw a prostitute. I saw a beautiful girl. I had to remind myself I was there to write a book, and somehow stay pure in the process. In that moment, I wasn't sure if I was about to be a customer, an author, or what.

Ava led me to her bed. I took a seat. It was cluttered with stuffed animals and reminded me of Sarah's bed from the Mustang Ranch, except Sarah's bed was softer. Ava's bed was more like a massage table with a sheet on it, and looked like a coffin. It was clinical and not intended for long sleeps. I nervously sat on the edge with my legs dangling as if in a doctor's office. The room smelled a bit like a doctor's office too, with a twist. Ava flung herself down and rubbed up against me.

"So, what do you want to know for this book?" she asked.

"Everything," I responded.

Ava slid off the bed, walked to her vanity to spray perfume and apply lip-gloss, and returned. Curling up next to me, while unlacing her boots, she whispered, "When I moan during sex, I usually fake it. Guys like to hear a woman moan. The problem is, sometimes my mind wanders and I forget. When I see the customer is not going to cum, I start again. If I like the guy, like I like you, I don't need to fake it. It comes naturally. If I don't like the guy, and he's going to be a quickie, I keep my boots on. They're too much of a pain to take off for fifteen minutes."

"When did you first start working?" I asked.

"Questions, questions, questions," she said, rubbing her nose against mine. "As my boots are off, why don't I show you what I do for a living? You can put that in your book."

"How about we just talk about it," I said.

"Talking makes me tired," she said. "What's to know? I fuck for a living, and I'm great at it. Here, let me show you," she said, placing my hand on her breast. "How does that feel?" she asked.

In that moment, sure, I wanted to be with her. On one hand, a voice inside me said, *Fuck it, I'm already behind a window, why not go all the way? I'm halfway there. Go big or go home. No one will ever know.* Something made me stop. Despite being behind a window, and partially seduced by its power, the illusion was gone. The district preys on fantasy. The veil had been lifted.

But there was something else, and that surprised me most of all. It was a sense of loyalty to Emma. If I was going to break my vow and sleep with a prostitute, it was going to be with her, not some random girl. I worked hard to build trust with Emma over the past few months. I was not about to break it. How could I say no to her, only to spend 50 guilders on another? In my mind, it didn't seem right. At that moment, for the first time, I realized how strong my feelings for Emma had become. It scared the shit out of me.

"You feel amazing, Ava, but I can't do this," I said, removing my hand from her breast. "It's complicated. Can we exchange numbers and talk sometime?"

Ava thought about it for a second, and said, "Fine, but only if you can count to ten in Dutch."

"Huh?" I responded.

"Yep. If you can't, I'll teach you."

She opened a drawer in her vanity and pulled out 10 condoms. Sitting on her bed with her legs spread open, she counted to 10, throwing a condom between her thighs with every number. "*Één, twee, drie, vier, vijf, zes, zeven, acht, negen, tien.* Now, it's your turn," she said.

It took me several tries to get it right. With each attempt, she inched closer. Soon, she was just about sitting in my lap. She placed one of her hands between her legs and the other high on my thigh, purring, "Now, how shall we celebrate?"

"How about by exchanging numbers?" I said.

"Fine," she said coldly, "but if you want to talk, it'll cost you."

In the end, Ava was no different from the rest. It was all business. Everything else was just a ploy to draw me in. That night, it almost worked. Ava got up from her bed and opened her curtain. I walked outside, defeated. I didn't take her number. No need. Ava was no more interested in my book than she was in her customers. She couldn't care less.

Ten minutes passed, and it was time to check on Michelle. Her curtain was drawn when I arrived, so I leaned up against a wall and waited for her next availability. After five minutes her door opened and a young man stumbled out. He seemed angry, flashed a thumbs-down, and scurried off. Michelle called me over.

"That guy's an asshole," she said. "He ran out of money and wanted to keep going. What do I look like? A social worker?" Michelle flashed a smile and slipped her phone number into my pocket. "Sure you don't want to come in? You won't regret it."

"I'll call you soon," I said, as we parted ways.

Overwhelmed by the night's adventures, I needed to mellow out before heading home. After all, that was the purpose of my stroll from the beginning. As there's no better place to chill than in a coffeeshop, I stumbled into The Grasshopper, bought a gram of Northern Lights and rolled myself a joint. That night, I had come closer than ever to fucking a prostitute. The one thing that ultimately held me back was Emma. My head was spinning.

I finished the joint and walked in the light rain to my bike. With so much on my mind, I wasn't ready to head home. Not directly. It was time for a late-night pedal through the city.

Biking through any European city in the still of the night is transcendent. Doing so in Amsterdam is divine.

While beautiful, it can be dangerous. Tram tracks, high curbs, metal posts, and cobblestones can turn a glorious pedal into a nightmare. The streets were quiet, but I needed to be careful, especially in the rain.

Given the night's adventures, it felt good moving through space. I needed to feel the elements. I needed to feel alive. I took a loop through the city, crossing illuminated bridges and canals, and passing the Anne Frank House, the Rijksmuseum, and Vondelpark. Nothing slowed my momentum as I glided through the air.

As I pedaled through town, I saw people in their homes eating, watching television, and engaging in all kinds of domestic activity. It was like looking into one fish tank after another. None of the homes had curtains or blinds. This held true for many homes in the city. Some say it's because the Dutch like light. Others say it's because of their Calvinist roots, showing the world they have nothing to hide. Others, yet, say it's because the Dutch are so cheap they refuse to spend money on window coverings. Regardless, it was refreshing to see such openness. While private in nature, the Dutch seemed to have no problem exposing their lives to anyone passing by.

I felt at peace on my bike, with the wind in my hair and gears clanking below. In that moment, with the energy of the city wrapped around me, and Northern Lights in my veins, I wanted to keep pedaling forever. My feeling of euphoria however was short lived. The drizzle turned into a downpour. After pedaling for 30 minutes, it was time to head home, and fast.

As I approached the central station, I made a sharp left amidst a snare of tram tracks. Just as I turned to admire the station, the front wheel of my bike wedged itself into a groove. That was all it took. With no time to react, I found myself flying through the air. It was a short flight and I hit the ground hard, landing on my wrists and knees. Bloodied, I got up, dusted myself off, fixed the handlebars, and pedaled home as if nothing happened. Just another night in Amsterdam.

Chapter 16

I CALLED MICHELLE several times over the next few days. The phone just rang. No answering machine. Nothing. Finally, she picked up.

"*Hallo,*" she said.

"Hi. It's David."

"Who?"

"The American from the other night."

"Who?" she repeated, confused.

"You know. The one working on the book."

"Oh, yeah," she remembered.

"How have you been?"

"Fine, I guess. I quit. It wasn't for me."

"That's great," I replied. "Now we can talk."

"I'm sorry. I can't. That's behind me, but good luck."

She hung up the phone. Another dead-end, same old story. Despite my efforts, no one was willing to help. That is, unless I paid them.

It had been days since I last saw Emma. I wasn't sure how to proceed. I had to be careful. At any moment she could simply say sorry, and that would be that. Maybe she would ask for money. That seemed to be how these women worked. Draw you in, until you have no choice but to say yes.

With Emma slow to return my calls, I walked past her window several times that week. I was eager to continue where we left off. We had a breakthrough at dinner, but now our momentum seemed lost. The first time I passed, her curtain was drawn. I came by a few days later, and same thing. Hoping she might be back soon, I wandered into The Grasshopper, smoked a joint, and meandered back. I had no expectation of seeing her, but was in no rush. I leaned against the wall and waited.

It started to rain, and I opened my umbrella. The crowds had thinned, and I gazed down Trompettersteeg, now dotted with puddles. Reflections from the red lights made the water glow like rubies, and as I listened to the sounds of rain against the chimes of the old church, it felt like I was part of a grand symphony, one that had been playing for centuries. It was some damn fine weed, that's for sure, and helped me appreciate the little things; things often overlooked that made up the fabric of the district.

As I stood there, immersed in all the sights and sounds, Emma's door opened. My heart pounded. A young man walked out. I nervously rushed over. From afar, something seemed different. Something seemed off. I couldn't place it. It was only when I got close that I realized what was going on. Another girl was standing in Emma's place.

My confusion turned to anger, and a feeling of betrayal. Had Emma left without telling me? The girl had the same hair and body type, but was definitely not her. Something was up. I wasn't happy about it. Although I prayed Emma would someday leave this world behind, she was my touchstone. I counted on her being there, at least for a few more weeks. With her gone, I felt exposed. I nicknamed the new girl The Imposter.

"Sorry, thought you were someone else," I said, standing face to face with the stranger.

"No problem," she responded. "How about I show you a good time?"

"I'm looking for a friend. Her name's Emma. She's usually here. Know her?" I asked with a sense of urgency.

"No, and who cares? You and I should become friends. Fifty guilders and I'll fuck you real good. Better than your friend. Promise."

"No thanks," I said, and left the district.

I pedaled home and called Emma. She didn't answer. I left a message. "Hey, Emma, it's David. Hope you're OK. Call me." I stretched out on my bed and listened as the No. 3 tram rumbled by. Once again I felt like a kid in high school, this time waiting for a girl to call. I virtually willed the phone to ring. It didn't.

Then it hit me. She might be gone for good. If she never returned to her window, or returned my calls, I would have no way of finding her. It would be almost as if she never existed. Just like that, without even knowing it, our time together might have run out. I passed her window several times that week. The Imposter was there every time. Emma was nowhere to be found.

A few days later I called again, just in case.

Astonishingly, she picked up.

"Hi, Emma," I said, overjoyed. "I've been trying to find you. How have you been?"

"Shitty," she replied sharply. "These are the questions you ask a prostitute?"

"I'm just saying hi," I said. "I was thinking about you, and worried. I went by your window. Someone else was there."

"Don't think too much about me, because I'm leaving. I'm moving to Tunisia. Tomorrow." It felt like someone had punched me in the gut.

"For how long?" I asked.

"A while," she said. "So, it was nice meeting you. Sorry I couldn't help. You can try me in a few weeks if you want. I might be back, but probably not." She was cold and distant, and made me think our entire relationship was in my mind.

"Goodbye, Emma," I said, with nothing left to say.

"Goodbye," she replied. "And please, don't waste your time worrying about me. I'm just a prostitute, remember?"

With that, after countless hours roaming the district and knocking on windows, I had nothing. Except, perhaps, a bruised heart. Emma was off to Africa and might never return. Even if she did, she seemed to lack enthusiasm for my book, and for me. Regardless, I would likely be in America by then. It turned out Oliver was right. These girls didn't want to talk, especially to an American writing a book. Like so many others, I had become lost in the fantasy, my fantasy. I had fallen under its spell. While I felt my journey was still worthwhile, it was a huge letdown. I knocked on Oliver's door to tell him the news. It would surely come as a disappointment. He was hoping I would do the impossible.

"She's gone, Oliver," I said. "I came close, but she's gone."

"I told you," he replied. "These women only care about money. Nothing else. But you accomplished more than I thought possible."

"Yeah, I guess," I replied. "But I feel like shit. I was starting to really care about her."

"That's what they do. They get guys to care," Oliver said. "She was just doing her job."

At this point, any attempt to return to the district was futile. I had exhausted my resources. However, the one place I hadn't explored was a brothel. I knew the culture there was different, perhaps more hospitable. I figured this would be my last attempt, my final hurrah, and then I'd call it quits. Just like in Nevada, I would visit, grab a drink, and gain perspective. But I needed someone to come with me.

After my close encounter with Ava, I questioned my resolve. The less likely the book became, the more likely it seemed I might sleep with a prostitute. Ultimately, the book and my feelings for Emma were the two main things holding me back. With both of them gone, I had no idea what I might do. Taking a friend would provide a line of defense. I would no longer be anonymous.

"No way," Oliver said defensively. "I can't go there."

"It's fine," I replied. "It's for research. Let's grab a drink, nothing more. It'll be interesting."

Oliver looked at me sadly, and said, "It's time to give up."

"How about this," I countered, knowing Oliver had been coveting the Purple Rocket. "If I promise to give you my bike when I leave Amsterdam, will you come?"

"The locks, too?" he asked.

"The locks, too," I replied. "Let's do it!"

"You mean tonight?" he said, his voice cracking.

"No time like the present."

"Fine," he conceded. "I just need to prepare."

"Prepare for what?" I asked, laughing. "We're going to a brothel. You look fine. Let's go."

"No, I need to get ready," he insisted, and proceeded to shower and groom himself as if going on a date. After 20 minutes, he was ready to go.

The first thing we needed was to figure out where we were going. Back in the day, we couldn't just jump on the Internet. Instead, we grabbed a copy of the daily paper *De Telegraaf*, flipped to the classified ads, and found the listings. Most of the clubs were clustered in the upscale museum district, and we limited our list to those places that didn't charge a cover. We found a map, located the clubs, and planned our attack. Our first stop would be Societe Anonyme.

We headed south, pedaling over bridges and through the chimes of the Westerkerk. These were the same chimes Anne Frank heard from her attic and found so reassuring despite the Nazis swarming below. As I lived a few blocks away, I routinely pedaled past her house. Every time, I would get the chills. Just 60 years earlier, Anne lived on the same streets in different times. Horrible times. Having now lived in her neighborhood for months, her story became personal.

Reading her diary in America was one thing. To breathe the same air, and hear the same sounds, was something else.

As we flew past her house that night, tears filled my eyes as I reflected on how different the world was from when she was struggling to survive, and how society's reluctance to stand up to evil cost Anne her life, and almost destroyed the world in the process. Despite everything, Anne wrote, "I don't think of all the misery, but of all the beauty that still remains." Her words provided me with focus throughout my time in Holland, and perspective. As we crossed the Amstel River that night, I was overcome by the heaviness of history in the air.

Once we reached the Rijksmuseum, we made a left and continued in the direction of the Heineken Factory. The night was still, and the streets were ours. Soon, we arrived at our first destination, a wood house bereft of any signs or markings except a row of red lanterns. We chained our bikes to a post across the street and approached. Oliver followed a few paces behind.

It was 11 o'clock when we rang the buzzer. The door clicked open and we walked up a flight of wood stairs to a small nondescript bar. Oliver and I took a seat at the counter, nervously looking around the room. While waiting for our drinks, I practiced my new language skills by counting the girls in the brothel. I was throwing down Dutch digits like a pro, and Oliver was digging it, although he did make a correction or two. For the most part, Ava had taught me well.

Unlike the Mustang Ranch, there was no lineup when we arrived. No souvenir stand. No fanfare whatsoever. Two

German businessmen sat on a couch sipping whisky, and a few women were scattered around the room. None of them seemed happy to see us. For the most part they were unattractive, the kind you might find hanging around a Greyhound bus station. Compared to the women of the De Wallen, they seemed less enthusiastic about their jobs—if that was even possible.

Halfway through my beverage, we had yet to be approached by anyone. It felt like we had wandered into a private party uninvited. I told Oliver we would finish our drinks and move on. Taking my final sip, I made eye contact with the most attractive girl in the room. She was sitting on a couch by herself. She looked at me, stood up, and walked over. We remained seated as she approached. We were excited one of the women was finally giving us the time of day. Our excitement quickly turned to fear.

Yelling so loud everyone could hear, she shrieked, "So you are the butcher and we are the pieces of meat? Pick us apart. Like our tits? Like our ass? You disgust me. We know what you're thinking."

This was the last thing we expected to hear at a brothel. After she finished her tirade, the room became quiet, everyone awaiting our response. Oliver looked at the ground, trying to make himself invisible. After a short pause, I replied, "No, that's not what we're thinking. You got us all wrong. We aren't looking for trouble, or trying to be disrespectful. Why the attitude?"

"Why the attitude?" she asked. "Why the fuck are you here, as clearly you don't want to do any fucking."

"It's our first time. We're just checking it out."

"Well, check this out," she said, flashing her pussy. "Come fuck, or get the fuck out. You've been here fifteen minutes. This is a brothel, not a zoo."

Figuring what the hell, I responded with "je bent zo mooi," hoping to charm her with my Dutch.

"That's all you got?" she snapped, unimpressed.

"Well, I can count to ten. Want to hear?"

She didn't, and stormed off.

Oliver, not one for confrontation, tugged on my shirt to leave. I agreed, and we made our exit. However, once we got to the door, there was no way out. The door had no handle. We were trapped. Oliver started breathing heavily as I walked back up the stairs to ask for help. Before I could say a word, the angry girl said, "Can't open the door, can you? I guess you need our services after all." Letting out a sick laugh, she pressed a hidden button. "Next time you come to a brothel, come to fuck, not sightsee or practice your Dutch," she said as the door clicked open.

We climbed on our bikes and did our best to put the fiasco behind us. It wasn't easy. Oliver was ready to go home. Societe Anonyme was advertised as one of the most luxurious and versatile brothels in the city, where every fantasy could come true. If my fantasy was to be verbally abused by an unhinged prostitute in a crowded room, they nailed it. After some pleading, Oliver agreed to come with me to the next stop on our list, Club Elegance. Hopefully things would be different there.

Although the club was only a few blocks away, we got lost finding it. After biking in circles in the light mist, we stopped pedaling alongside a canal.

"Let's see if someone can help," I said.

"No way!" Oliver exclaimed. "We can't ask a stranger for directions to a brothel."

"Come on," I urged, and approached a Dutchman walking a golden retriever. The guy had heard of the place, but didn't know its location.

Five minutes later, we saw a young couple holding hands. Oliver urged me not to intrude. "They're on a date. You can't ask them," he said.

I pedaled over. "Excuse me. We're lost. Do you know where we can find Club Elegance?"

He paused for a second, looked at his girl, and pointed to a building directly behind us. "We just came from there. You're standing in front of it," he said.

We turned around, and there it was. There were no red lights marking the place, only a silver plaque by the door. We rang the doorbell just before midnight. A doorman took our jackets, handed us a ticket, and asked if we arrived by taxi. We said no. If we had, it would have cost us, as the brothel would have imposed a cover charge to pay the driver for dropping us off.

The first thing we noticed was the building itself. It was built in the mid-nineteenth century and was stunning. It was like walking into an elegant home, a far cry from our last stop. Once atop the stairs, we found ourselves in a large Victorian-era sitting room, complete with sophisticated couches and rugs. There were women everywhere, and a few men. We made our way to the bar and ordered a drink.

Almost immediately, an attractive Spanish girl sat down beside us. She barely spoke English, and when she did, had a thick Castilian lisp. We tried striking a conversation. It wasn't easy. Her English was rough, and my Spanish was limited to repeating phrases I had picked up while backpacking through Spain, such as "*Donde esta el ayuntamiento*," and "*Los pollitos dicen pio pio pio*." While useful on the streets, the phrases weren't particularly helpful in a brothel. She had no idea where city hall was, and wasn't interested in chicken.

After a few failed attempts at communicating, she asked us to buy her a drink. That, I could clearly understand. It was a phrase she had been practicing. I said no, and she excused herself.

As she walked away, I made eye contact with a gorgeous dark-skinned girl sitting by herself at a table. She had the look of a dancer. For a second, I forgot where I was and flirted with her as though she was a normal girl. I smiled. She smiled back. I blushed. The usual. I left Oliver at the bar and sat down by myself on a couch, hoping she would join. She did.

"My name's Julia," she said with a Dutch accent.

"I'm David. Nice to meet you," I replied.

"Thanks for letting me join," she said humbly. "I've only worked here a month. I still get nervous. Is this your first time?"

"Yeah," I said.

"Where are you from?" she asked.

"California."

"Really? I've always dreamed of going there. Maybe you can take me someday."

"Maybe," I said, admiring her beauty.

"What brings you to Amsterdam?" she asked.

"I'm working on a book about the district."

Her eyes lit up. "Really? Can I be in your book?" she asked.

"I'd love that," I said.

"Great! Let's get some champagne first and fuck."

"Ah, I wish. I'm not here for that."

"Come on," she said. "You're a man. I'm a woman. I'll treat you right. Let's start with a piccolo," referring to a small bottle.

"I'm good," I said again.

"Are you sure?" she persisted. "Buy a girl a drink."

"No thanks," I answered, tired of the hustle.

"OK, how about we just go to a private room? I like you. We can start by taking a bath, and then I'll give you the best massage of your life. That's what Amsterdam is all about."

"You're beautiful, and I'd love to," I replied, "but I'm here to write a book, not become a customer." My usual line, once again.

"Oh, well, maybe some other time," she replied. "*Doei.*"

Julia got up and returned to her friends. As she told them what happened, they laughed.

I continued sitting on the couch, wondering what I was doing in a brothel. Soon, I returned to check on Oliver. He remained sitting where I left him, and looked traumatized. While I was gone, several women had made their way over. One by one, Oliver graciously denied their advances, which included the usual, "I really like you," "There's something special between us," "This is my first week," and, "You seem different."

There's only so long you can sit at a bar in a brothel. We'd already learned that the hard way. This club proved no different, and soon the manager started flashing dirty looks. We finished our drinks and called it a night. Overall we had a fine experience at our second stop, at least comparatively, but Julia was just like the others. She would entertain my fantasy of helping with the book, but only to seduce me.

The next night, Oliver and I set out to explore the final brothel on our list. It was Club Jan Bik, conveniently located a few blocks from our building off Haarlemmerstraat. I had passed by the place countless times, never noticing it. This was our neighborhood brothel, and maybe the cheapest in Amsterdam.

We arrived at six o'clock on a Sunday night, not exactly rush hour. After quickly securing our bikes, we knocked on the door and were greeted by a manager named Melissa. She said the club was empty, but we should come upstairs and wait. She would keep us company.

The place was less than spectacular, and nothing like Club Elegance. The main room was small and cluttered, and the furniture looked like the kind you might find abandoned on a sidewalk. Several of the sofas were so old they were covered in dirty bed sheets, dotted with cigarette burns. When I told Melissa I was working on a book, she insisted we wait until the girls arrived. She was only the manager and couldn't help, but maybe one of the girls could. So, we waited, and talked, and watched as a black cat leaped around the room.

The first to show up was Cathy, a thick blonde from England with huge red lips—and they weren't just red because of her lipstick. In addition to a mushrooming pimple on her forehead, she had a festering red sore on her upper lip, partially scabbed over. As she talked, the scab clung to her lip like a rock climber clinging to a cliff during a snowstorm. It was hypnotic, and fucking horrible.

"I'm always happy here. This is my home," Cathy said, applying another layer of lipstick. "Lately, I've been getting so much work. Lawyers, doctors, politicians, they all come to see me. I'll tell you what you want to know for your book. But let's fuck first." There it was, the same old line, right on cue.

"All I want to do is talk," I replied.

"Too bad," Cathy said, as she threw herself on a couch and tossed her legs in the air. "You should enjoy yourself a little."

"I know. I'm working on it."

"One little fuck. Come on. They say I'm the best."

The doorbell rang, and Melissa rushed downstairs to greet her guest. A Japanese man walked in and pointed to Cathy. It was an easy choice. She was the only hooker in the room. Cathy went behind the bar, grabbed a stack of towels and a handful of condoms, and disappeared upstairs. The man followed.

Melissa, Oliver, and I spent the next several hours listening to music and talking about life and love. We explained we visited a few other brothels and confronted a lot of anger.

"Not here. Only love here," Melissa said. "When you're angry, it's because you see yourself as a victim. We're not victims here. We refuse."

"That's powerful stuff," I replied, reflecting on the wisdom of her words in Amsterdam's cheapest brothel.

"Yeah, someone told me that once. Always remembered it."

"Amazing what you remember, and what you don't," I replied, as we became lost in our thoughts.

Cathy went up and down the stairs three times, servicing an elderly Dutch man, a young English kid, and the Japanese guy. No other women were working that night. She even tried a few more times to get our business, going as far as offering a two-for-one with Oliver.

After eating far too many peanuts at the bar, we announced our departure. Melissa gave us a hug and told us to come by anytime for a drink. We were welcome there. Oliver was touched, and felt like he'd made a friend. We then said goodbye to Cathy.

"Next time we'll talk and fuck," she said, with the scab still dangling from her lip.

"Yeah, sure. Next time," I said, knowing I would never see her again. While glad we checked out the brothel scene, it was readily apparent I would find little, if any, help there.

Once outside, it felt good to be breathing the fresh air. But feelings change fast, especially in Amsterdam, and Oliver's did. When we went around the corner to unlock our bikes, Oliver let out a scream. The inevitable had happened.

"Mother fucker!" he yelled down the Dutch streets. The Purple Rocket was still there, but Oliver's bike was gone. Vanished. All that was left was the front tire, still locked to a post. Caught up in the excitement of things, he forgot to secure the frame.

"Well, at least you get the Purple Rocket soon," I said, letting out a chuckle. "Now, I'll even let you rename it the Red Rocket."

"Mother fucker," he repeated in a thick Dutch accent, as he climbed on the back of my bike and I pedaled the two of us home.

Chapter 17

WITH MY TIME in the district behind me, I lived the life of a normal exchange student in Amsterdam, more or less. I attended class, visited museums, picnicked in Vondelpark, and even took a tour on a canal boat. Mornings were spent in Squash City, working out and hitting the sauna. Afternoons were spent studying, and evenings largely consisted of drinking with Oliver and my university friends, chilling at our favorite coffeeshops, and dancing at Amsterdam's popular nightclubs, particularly Melkweg, a converted dairy factory, and Paradiso, a former church. We even enjoyed drinks at Dansen Bij Jansen, Amsterdam's infamous student nightclub. Drum and bass music was huge back then and boomed everywhere we went.

Other than my layover in Iceland and trip to Oktoberfest, I had stayed in Holland the entire semester. Now, with Emma in Africa, there was nothing keeping me in town. That is, other than my one day of class. So, after a long Thursday at university, I decided it was time to pick up my copy of *Let's Go Europe* and do some backpacking. I had six days to see the world.

Nothing compares to the feeling of standing in a European train station, looking at the overhead destination display, and deciding where you want to wake up next—Paris, Prague, Berlin, Bratislava, Moscow, or wherever. When backpacking without a fixed agenda, you can travel in any direction you choose, at a moment's notice, to cities you have only dreamed of. It's a feeling of total freedom and discovery, and can be addictive. Especially when traveling alone.

When backpacking solo, you don't just travel the world. You become part of it. You have no choice but to live in the moment. Your survival depends on it, and there can be great communion as a result. Nothing can be taken for granted, from finding food and shelter, to securing safe passage. The basic necessities of life, so often overlooked, become all that matters.

Traveling with friends can be great. But when alone, you are immersed in the culture, and have no one to rely on but yourself. All your senses are blazing. You notice the details, and life is put in perspective. As Marcel Proust explains, "The real voyage of discovery consists not in seeking new landscapes, but in having new eyes." Those eyes are opened to the fullest when flying solo.

Sure, it can be lonely, but there are always friendships to make and adventures to be had. The true joy of backpacking is more about the relationships you develop than the places you visit. Individual paths cross, converge, and then separate, just like when I was in Iceland. Friendships develop fast. There is a sense of urgency, and something special shared. Something fleeting but transformative, that will forever be etched in your sense of self.

As Oliver was bikeless, I lent him the Purple Rocket until I returned. He had been suffering without a bike for days, and I felt partially responsible. I also remembered what life was like in Holland without a bike, like a bird remembering life before it could fly. He was appreciative and promised to be careful.

I said goodbye to Oliver and the Purple Rocket, hoping to see both of them again, and took a taxi to the central station where I bought a ticket to Maastricht. After touring the famous caves, I moved on to Luxembourg City and then Interlaken. Once in Switzerland, I checked into Balmers Hostel, a popular spot for backpackers, and selected from a list of activities. I only had time for two excursions, and had to choose wisely. First, I went paragliding over the Swiss Alps. Next, I took the Jungfraubahn railway to the highest train station in Europe, 11,332 feet above sea level. It was refreshing to be in nature and surrounded by such awe-inspiring beauty. It felt like I was on top of the world. Amsterdam seemed a lifetime away.

After two nights hanging out at Balmers with backpackers from around the world, I took the train to Liechtenstein to get my passport stamped, and proceeded to Salzburg where I checked into the Yoho International Hostel, another highly trafficked haunt. Before even making it to my room, four Americans wearing matching red and white skirts came running over.

"Hurry up and let's go," one of them said, panting. "We're leaving now. We have room for one more."

"Sounds cool," I replied, delirious from my travels. "Where to?"

"The country. It'll be fun."

At that point, the only thing I wanted was a bed. The train to Salzburg was packed, and I stood the entire way. My ankles were killing me. Moreover, I hadn't slept in 36 hours. I was nearing the point of collapse, but there were new experiences to be had. It was time to push on.

Before I knew it, I was in the back of a minivan headed for the Austrian hills. The girls were nice and the van comfortable. We were off to a good start. After leaving city limits, the driver began playing the soundtrack to *The Sound of Music*. All four girls sang along. They were sopranos, except for one, who was an alto. As for me, I had only seen the movie once, and wasn't really a fan.

Then I figured it out. This was no ordinary tour of the country. On the contrary, this was a special *The Sound of Music* tour. During the next six hours, the driver played the soundtrack over and over while the girls sang along to every note. The van only stopped when we arrived at a location from the movie. Being the only guy, I was obliged to act out every scene.

We visited the Mirabell Gardens, the Hellbrunn Palace gazebo, and various other spots. The driver played all the standards, including "Sixteen Going on Seventeen" and "Do-Re-Mi." The girls' favorite thing to sing, unquestionably, was, "How Do You Solve a Problem Like Maria?" They sang this everywhere, in between each and every location, as if trying to break a record. It felt like I had been taken hostage. Amidst all this, Emma was still very much on my mind. The contrast between her world, and that of these girls, was painful. They were roughly the same age, and oh what a different life they lived.

The six-hour adventure culminated with us stopping in Mondsee, the site of the von Trapp wedding. One of the girls started crying. I wanted to cry as well. After eating a slice of strudel, we headed back. When backpacking, you never know where you will end up, and not knowing is ultimately what makes the journey so worthwhile.

It's hard to admit, but the tour became a highlight of my time in Europe. Maybe, though, that's because one of the girls took a liking to me, and I to her. Over the next few days, we became lost in our own fairy tale, touring the Hohensalzburg Fortress, visiting Mozart's birthplace, and attending a concert of *Ave Maria* in St. Peter's Church. Finally, with school calling, it was time to board the night train to Amsterdam and say goodbye. Standing at the station, we parted ways without even knowing each other's last name. Those moments were all we were meant to share.

It had only been a week, but I was nervous as the train pulled into the station. I was afraid of getting swept back into the district. I was also afraid I might never see the Purple Rocket again. Oliver did get his last bike stolen. I prepared for the worst. Sure enough, the two of us were reunited.

After a long day at university, I pedaled home to do some schoolwork. Final exams were approaching. I read for comparative criminology, wrote an essay for international dispute settlement, and then spontaneously decided to call Emma. She was likely still in Tunisia, but it had been several weeks. Incredibly, she picked up.

"*Hallo*," she answered.

"Hi, Emma. It's David."

"Oh, hi. I'm back from Africa," she said distantly. Her plan had fallen through, and she was back at work. "Once a whore, always a whore," she said, filling me in on her time away.

"When can I see you?" I asked, in disbelief I was hearing her voice.

"Not until Monday. I have to work."

"Great," I replied. "Let's grab a bite and talk about the book."

"Dinner is fine," she said. "But I'm not sure I have time for your book."

"Our book," I replied. "Whatever time you have will be fine."

As I hung up the phone, I felt lost. The district was drawing me in, once again. What the hell was I doing? Was there really a book here, or did I just enjoy the company of a beautiful girl? I had focused so hard on a goal for so long, I no longer knew what I was trying to accomplish. However I was not about to give up, regardless of the reason or result. I still believed in Emma. I remembered how she looked at me the first time we met. Our connection was real. I knew that to be true, and Emma wanted to keep our story going—if only for a bit longer. Just as I was looking for answers, she seemed to be as well. Maybe, I could help her find what she was looking for.

Chapter 18

WHEN MONDAY CAME, I wanted to look my best. The problem was, my wardrobe was limited. I had few options, having long since retired my Eurotrash outfit. The nicest thing I owned was a Brooks Brothers shirt and slacks. That would have to do. I looked right out of a law school catalogue, but so be it. It was time to go preppy.

It was a crisp Dutch night when I set out to meet her. Winter was in the air, and the millennium was knocking on the door. I pedaled past the Anne Frank House and several coffeeshops before arriving in Dam Square, which had already been converted into a carnival for the holidays. The square was filled with people drinking mulled wine, going on rides, listening to music, and shopping.

With time to kill, I took a ride on the Ferris wheel. As I went round and round in the chilly air, I marveled at the views and reflected on my journey. Soon I would be gone and Amsterdam would be little more than a dream. I had two weeks left. My time was almost up. For the moment, I was still in that dream. I had not yet awoken, and had moments left to create. Looking down at the lights, my mind was overcome with feelings of peace and urgency.

When the ride came to an end, I locked the Purple Rocket in Dam Square and walked past the Hotel Krasnapolsky into the district. The plan was to meet Emma at Lunch Room 52. But plans change, especially in the district, and I strolled by her window to see if she was around.

Just as I approached, her curtain opened. There she was, wearing a red silk gown. We stood momentarily and looked at each other like we did the first time we met. It started to rain. Emma opened her door.

"You look nice," she said, "but you're going to get soaked. Here, why don't you come in?"

"OK," I said, just like that.

I stepped inside, and Emma closed the curtain behind us.

Having spent so much time on the outside, it felt like a threshold had been crossed. The die had been cast. *Alea iacta fuerat.* I knew my actions would have consequences. With two weeks left, I didn't care. It might sound cliché, but when a door opens, you go through it. Otherwise you might end up standing in the cold. But this was no ordinary door—of that, I was well aware.

Emma took my hand and led me up a spiral staircase to a room shrouded in red light. A basket of condoms sat by a sink. I sat on the bed and tried not to think about how many guys she had fucked on it. Emma joined me and lit a cigarette. It felt good being in her company. I felt safe. I had imagined being behind Emma's window, but not like this. I was there as a friend, not a customer.

"I'm in a real shit mood. Real shit," Emma said.

"What's wrong?" I asked the 24-year-old prostitute.

"Major credit card debt to start, and things have been slow," she said with resignation. "I've been earning about five hundred guilders a day. Total shit. This is the slow season. Guys are saving up for Christmas. All the girls are complaining."

After a short pause, I said, "I have an idea that might help."

"Yeah?" she asked.

"Promise not to laugh."

"Fine," she said.

"Ever wear a man's shirt in your window?" I asked. "You know, with nothing else?"

"Why the hell would I do that?" she responded.

"I haven't seen anyone try that look. You'll stand out."

"You think?"

"Go for it. There are few things sexier than waking up to a beautiful girl wearing your shirt from the night before, perhaps making breakfast."

"I don't cook for any guy," she snapped.

"I'm not talking about cooking. I'm talking about you making money," I said as I unbuttoned my Brooks Brothers shirt and handed it to her, leaving me in a white T-shirt. "Another gift."

"I don't need more gifts," she replied.

"Fine. Borrow it then," I said softly.

Emma stood up, flashed a smile, and took the shirt. I assumed she would save it for later. I assumed wrong. Without saying more, she loosened the straps of her gown. It slid down her body and fell to the floor.

Standing only in her underwear and my necklace, she said, "Well, I have to try it on." She then walked back and forth like in a fashion show. "Don't need this anymore," she said, unbuckling her bra and tossing it on the bed. "How do I look?"

"Eh . . . perfect," I replied.

She then proceeded to tell me she had just done a line of coke and was thinking about killing herself.

"I'm finished with being a prostitute. I just need something to make me stop. But I've been saying that for years, so whatever," she said dismissively. "It's a lonely life. In truth, after work, I hate going home to an empty space. I haven't had a real boyfriend in years. My last boyfriend became my pimp. He called again today, begging me to come back. Yeah, right. I don't want to be a prostitute forever. I want a house and a husband who loves me."

Somehow, Emma was still able to dream.

She continued, "I was going to manage a restaurant in Utrecht for a customer. I was going to get away from all this, but he just had to fall in love with me. He calls all the time now, and wants to know where I live. Forget it. Now I can't see my number one customer anymore. It's all crap."

As I listened to Emma, the sounds of men outside punctuated my thoughts and brought me back to reality. Lying on her bed, I never wanted to face that reality. I didn't want Emma to either.

"Tunisia was the best," she continued. "People are nice, even if you're a prostitute. No one makes money, but life is good. Unlike here."

"Ah, come on. Don't be so negative," I said. "Life's all about perspective. There's no reality but what we create for ourselves."

"Yeah, right! Like this isn't real?" she said, pointing at the basket of condoms. "Like those guys outside, they aren't real?"

"Sorry," I said, knowing I'd gone too far.

"No. It's fine," she said gently. "I like how you talk to me. You care. That's something new."

In that moment, I wanted nothing more than to hold Emma in my arms. I wanted to be with her. Lying on her bed, I was more attracted to her than ever. There I was, alone in the district, thousands of miles from home. A part of me wanted to throw her down and do what I had been thinking about for months, but mostly refused to acknowledge.

There was no denying that since meeting Emma, she was always on my mind. Now, she was in front of me. Surely she would accept my money, if it came down to that. That was her job. Yes, the book would be compromised. I would become a customer, breaking my rule. However, at that moment, I wondered what I was even doing with my book. Until recently, I had no expectation of ever seeing Emma again. After tonight, I had every reason to believe she would disappear on me once more.

What held me back wasn't the book, or the smell of latex that consumed the room, or the sounds of men below. What held me back were my feelings for Emma. When I looked at her, I no longer saw a prostitute. I saw a friend, and someone I cared about. I saw a girl who was willing to take a chance on me, and trust me when she had no reason to. I took her faith in me seriously, and was moved by it. When it came to my desires, I wanted her for her. If we were to ever be together, it could never be behind a window. I knew that. But, watching her stretch out on her bed in my unbuttoned shirt, the temptation was stronger than ever. It was virtually consuming me alive.

"You know, I'll never marry a Dutchman," she said. "They're thin, cheap, and bad in bed."

"I'll take your word for it," I said, laughing.

"Maybe we should get married then," she said unexpectedly.

Not knowing what to say, but knowing she was teasing, I replied, "Emma, I'm too much of an optimist for you."

"Opposites attract," she said.

"Apparently," I said, blushing. I remained speechless as we stared into each other's eyes. I knew she was just flirting. That's what prostitutes do. But I wondered if there was something more. I wondered if I was beginning to mean something to her too.

Notwithstanding our time together, I knew little about her. I couldn't begin to imagine her story, and how she got to this place. Hopefully she would find time to share it.

We had been in her room for an hour when the phone rang. In my mind it seemed like 10 minutes. It's true what they say. Time passes differently when behind a window. For men, it goes by fast. For women, it creeps to a halt.

Emma stood up and took the call. It was her best friend Sophie, and they started talking in Dutch. Sophie was upset, and Emma did her best to calm her. From what I understood, she was having trouble getting her Tunisian boyfriend into Europe, and needed money.

With Emma preoccupied, I stretched out on her bed, resting my head on a white towel next to a jar of lube, and began playing with a string of beads hanging from the ceiling. Emma pushed them aside, explaining if I pulled the string a guard would rush in. Having seen how security does its job, I gave a sigh of relief.

Emma finished the call and sat down on the edge of her bed. She seemed removed and vacant. Then, out of nowhere, she burst into tears. I had seen her tear up before, but never like this.

"I'm sorry, I can't do dinner," she said. "I was looking forward to it, but I can't. I need money. I need to help my friend Sophie."

Rather than going to dinner, Emma had decided to go back to work. She needed to make money. But this time, it wasn't for her. It was for her friend. I couldn't believe it. Given the circumstances, it might have been the nicest thing I've ever seen anyone do. It was certainly the most selfless.

Not knowing what to do, I gave her a hug. I needed for us to be close, and for her to feel love. Emma got up and walked over to a mirror. She applied some makeup as she wiped away her tears, and then slipped out of my shirt and back into her dress.

"Don't want to give it a try?" I asked.

"Not tonight," she said.

"If you're still interested, we should work on the book," I said hesitantly. "I only have a few days left."

"Yes, your book." She took a breath, and said, "Why don't you come to my place next week? We can work on it there. But I'm not much of a writer you know."

"Really?" I asked in disbelief.

"Really," she replied.

Finally, it was happening. She was letting me in, but I never imagined it would be in her home. The thought never crossed my mind. That was a world she kept separate. She was clear about that. I was excited, but scared. I had no idea what might happen when we were alone outside the district. I knew I would be tested. I wondered if she really wanted to work on the book, or had something else in mind. Mostly, though, I worried she would disappear like so many times before. I tried to keep things in perspective, but wanted nothing more than to believe.

For the moment, our time together was up. We walked downstairs, exchanged air kisses, and paused behind her curtain to hold hands. Somehow, in the heart of the red lights, there was innocence. There was goodness, and there was a sense anything was possible. For a few moments, we were just two souls, alive at the same time, connecting. The real world seemed miles away.

Once outside, the rain had stopped. The stars were out. Everything seemed clean and new, if only for a second. That second passed. As I turned to say goodbye, a bunch of men approached. "How was your fuck?" one of them asked, eager to have a go. I dropped my head and walked down Trompettersteeg as Emma went back to work.

Chapter 19

AS I WALKED down Trompettersteeg the whole world went to black and white. After absorbing all the sights, sounds, and smells from behind Emma's window, my senses were spent. It was a lot to process, and I had more questions than ever. How did this beautiful girl end up here? What makes her stay? What went wrong? Does she believe in redemption? Does she believe in God, and what would have happened if I tried to kiss her? All these questions flooded my mind, and more.

Never once did I try to save her, but now, all I could think about was doing so. Being behind her window changed things. I came face to face with the reality of her world. The horrors of the district were real, and Emma needed to get out before it was too late. For all I knew, she had already passed the point of no return.

I wasn't ready for our night to end. I wanted to run back and steal her away. We had made progress and broken through barriers. I wanted to break through more. Knowing I couldn't go back to her window, but wanting to be close, I stopped at the Green House coffeeshop and bought a gram of Northern Lights. I sat at the bar and rolled myself a joint.

Without question, I had smoked more weed since arriving in Amsterdam than in all my life combined. It was no big deal, just part of life. It centered me and helped me appreciate the moment, and reflect on the past. Sitting in the coffeeshop, I remembered the words Inga repeated my first night in town. "Amsterdam is in my heart. Amsterdam, it is life." Her words echoed in my mind as I walked outside to give Emma a call. I needed to hear her voice one more time before calling it a night.

After a few rings, she picked up.

"Can you call back in thirty minutes?" she asked.

"Sure," I said, leaving it at that.

I wandered through Dam Square, found my bike locked by the Ferris wheel, and pedaled to my apartment. Never in my wildest dreams did I imagine my time in Amsterdam would unfold as it had, or that I would develop feelings for a Dutch prostitute. Despite being so far along, I wasn't sure if my experiment would end in triumph or tragedy. I prayed something good would come of it all, and that my naivety and optimism wouldn't ultimately get the better of me.

When I arrived home, a party was taking place on the roof. Oliver was there, along with the usual international crowd. The song "Magic" by Ben Folds Five played as the group feasted on spaghetti carbonara and Bulgarian wine. I made myself a plate and looked out across the city in the direction of Emma's window. My eyes welled up with tears.

"You OK?" Oliver asked, putting his arm around me.

"Not sure," I replied. "I just spent the last hour with Emma, behind her window."

Oliver's jaw dropped. "You did what?"

"No, no," I replied. "We hung out as friends."

"What? Really? What's going on?"

"I don't know," I continued. "But it might be something special."

"She's a prostitute. Don't forget that," Oliver warned, feeling responsible for encouraging me.

Oliver was right. I needed to be careful, not only of my feelings, but of my safety. I had never been to the home of a prostitute before. Did she live in a rough part of town? What would happen once there? I remembered Emma had mentioned her ex, who was once her pimp. I knew he was lurking around. Maybe he had something planned. Anything was possible.

It had been over 30 minutes, so I disappeared and gave Emma a call.

"Hi, Emma."

"Hi," she replied, sad and lifeless.

"You should call it a night. I'm worried about you," I said.

"Don't worry until we're married," she said.

"Think that will ever happen?"

"You never know," she said.

"Well, let's finish the book. Then we can talk marriage," I replied, playing into things. After a long silence, I said, "Emma, you there?"

"I just don't know," she said tentatively. "I'm really busy. There's no time. Call in a few days. Things might change.

I'm sorry," she continued, as I heard a man's voice in the background. "I have a customer. Let's talk later."

"Emma, please," I pleaded. "I'm leaving soon. Your story matters. I just need a day."

"I have to go," she said mechanically, and hung up the phone.

After everything, Emma was getting cold feet. She was backing out, again. The promising night had turned into a disaster. My journey through the district had been exhausting. At the very least, it was relieving to know it was coming to an end.

The next day was Thanksgiving. A group of my American friends from grad school gathered in town for an expat feast. I studied with them in London. They had all stayed in Europe after graduation. I was the only one who returned home. I enjoyed expat life, almost became lost in it, and it felt good to be reunited. Whether I liked it or not, law school had changed me. Seeing them brought me back to an earlier time.

Celebrating American holidays abroad can be challenging, and finding a full-size turkey in Holland was no easy task. We planned ahead, and one of my friends traveled with one from England. Unable to afford the Eurotunnel, he made the 10-hour trip by way of train, bus, and ferry. Having spent so much time with the bird, albeit frozen, he grew attached to it. He named it Loretta, and delivered a short but heartfelt eulogy before we began our meal. Life in Europe was weird for sure. That's what made it so special.

After our feast, the group wanted to roam the district. My talking about the book got them excited. I decided to tag along. It was drizzling when we left. Soon, it became a deluge. Visibility was low and we hurried to find shelter. Then, it happened. I took a step, and my foot slipped— on a steaming pile of Amsterdam dog shit. "Goddamn it!" I yelled, as I scraped the crap off my shoe on the curb and caught up with the group. They had ducked into The Grasshopper. We smoked a joint of White Widow, and once the rain subsided, continued on our way.

Just like with the Indonesians months ago, I marched the group in a single file down Trompettersteeg into the De Wallen. It was early, and most of the curtains were drawn, including Emma's. My friends wanted to keep exploring. I didn't have it in me. After all the miles I put in, I had nothing left in the tank. I sat in Lunch Room 52 and ordered an espresso as the group wandered off without me. It had been a long day. I would catch up with them tomorrow.

Sipping my drink, I listened to the bells of the Oude Kerk. They had become the soundtrack for my time in Holland, but always made me uneasy. Since arriving in Amsterdam, I passed the church countless times. Never once did I enter. This was odd, as I loved cathedrals and toured many of them throughout Europe. Somehow, this church was different. It was majestic, but foreboding.

I noticed a side door was ajar, and something drew me in. As I walked across the street, the welcoming commit-tee worked hard to get my attention. These were the first women I had seen when exploring the district months ago. With The Scratcher doing her thing, I left the outside world behind and stepped into the oldest building in Amsterdam for the first time.

Immediately, a sensation of nausea overcame me. Then I felt a chill in the air, as if something bad had happened there. As I roamed around, I spent most of my time looking up at the windows. The place was empty and vacuous, organ music the only reminder there was life in the building. When I eventually looked down, a shiver ran through my spine. Underneath me were hundreds of tombstones. The place was a mass grave. More than 10,000 were buried there, including Vermeer and countless prostitutes. The church was literally built on the dead.

After a few minutes, I was ready to leave. On my way out, I glanced down one more time. Underneath me was a tombstone with two large cracks running through it. It had no name engraved into it, but it had a date. The date was my birthday. Freaked out, I got the fuck out of there. The church was even darker than I had imagined.

When I walked by Emma's window one last time, she was there, wearing my shirt and looking sexier than ever. But something seemed wrong. Her hair was tousled, and she was upset. She didn't greet me with a hug, but flashed a half-hearted smile, just like she would to a stranger.

"Nice shirt," I said.

"Yeah, it's working fine," she replied. "Why are you here?"

"It's American Thanksgiving. I have friends visiting, and they wanted to check out the district."

"Oh, I see," she continued. "I've never been to a Thanksgiving."

"Yeah, we sit around, eat turkey, and say what we're thankful for."

"Thankful? For what? This shit life?" Emma said quietly.

"You have much to be thankful for," I said.

"Yeah, right."

"As for me, I'd be thankful if you'd help with the book."

"Whatever you want," she said indifferently.

"Emma, this could be important."

"Why?" she asked.

"So something good could come from all this," I said, looking around the district. She nodded, tried to smile, but couldn't.

"Do you really believe that's possible?" she asked.

"I do. You matter." I paused, and continued, "Is the invitation still open?"

"Yes. Call me tomorrow," she said slowly. "But for now, I need to get back to work."

"Good night, Emma," I said.

"Good night, David, and don't do anything I wouldn't," she replied. "And that's not much."

Chapter 20

I CALLED EMMA the next morning and left a message. When I called again the following day, her phone stopped accepting messages. Sorry, mailbox full. Just like that, she had disappeared once again. With so few days left, it was likely for good.

Needing to clear my mind, Indonesian Mike, German Kyle, and I came together for one final adventure. We wanted to do something classically Dutch. We couldn't visit the tulips in Keukenhof. They weren't in bloom, so we did the next best thing. We headed to Zaanse Schans. It was an easy trip, and once there we were in awe. The windmills towered over the landscape like giants, a humbling reminder of how small we all are in the grand scheme of things. Mere specks in the breeze—but important specks, as the windmills couldn't have been built without us. Despite the terrifying realities of life, its fleeting nature, and the fact none of us have answers to life's most important questions, we matter. We count, and can make a difference. As I sat in the shadow of one of the windmills, taking it all in, I felt more grounded than I had in a while.

I spent my final hours in Amsterdam writing papers and studying for exams. I went by Emma's window a few times to say goodbye. Every time, a different girl stood in her place. I felt abandoned. I knew my journey was never within my control. Journeys never are, but my time in Holland felt incredibly incomplete.

After some studying, I aced my exams, said goodbye to my classmates, and began packing. Packing to leave a country you have come to love is never easy. Packing to leave the Netherlands is further complicated by having to make sure no weed-nugs hitchhike their way home. I heard too many stories of people getting busted for simply forgetting to check a pocket, and I carefully went through everything. I didn't want to finish my third year of law school as an international drug smuggler. Once I finished my sweep, I celebrated by smoking a joint of Jack, dumping the contents of my bag, and checking everything all over again. Say what you will about cannabis, but for me, one of the side effects is thoroughness.

With everything taken care of, I called Emma one last time. I had no expectation I would get through. She picked up, and seemed different.

"Hi, Emma, I've been trying to reach you," I said.

"I've been busy," she said tenderly.

"I wanted to say goodbye. I leave in two days."

"Do you still want that interview?" she asked hesitantly.

"Yes, but we're out of time."

"I've been thinking about what you said. You know, that something good can come from this," she said reflectively. "Can you come tomorrow?"

"That's perfect," I said, virtually speechless.

"I live outside Utrecht. Meet me at the Houten station at ten."

"Thanks for believing in me," I replied.

"I'm not sure about that," Emma said, "but I'll see you tomorrow."

I ran across the hall to tell Oliver the news. Sure enough, he was watching *The A-Team*. I walked in just as Colonel John "Hannibal" Smith uttered his famous line, "I love it when a plan comes together," and the closing music played. It was the perfect ending for my time in Holland, and a reminder of how far I'd come.

"Emma invited me to her home. I'm going tomorrow," I said. "She's finally going to help."

He froze. "Are you serious?"

"Yep."

"Where does she live?"

"Outside Utrecht."

"That's incredible, but be careful," he warned. "She's from a different world."

"I'll be fine," I replied.

"Things like this just don't happen in Holland."

"Well, it hasn't happened yet," I said, "so fingers crossed."

"Fingers crossed," he repeated.

The next morning I pedaled to the central station one last time. Saint Nicholas Day was upon us and the streets were filled with decorations—particularly life-size cutouts of *Sinterklaas* and the controversial *Zwarte Piet*. Once at the station, I looked for a place to secure my bike. It was easier said than done. Thousands of bikes crowded the racks. Eventually I found a spot. With a bit of luck, the Purple Rocket would be there when I returned.

I grabbed a coffee and made my way to the tracks. Standing on the platform, I once again had the feeling of being watched. I figured it was all in my mind, typical Amsterdam paranoia. But then, I saw him—the mystery man. Who the fuck was this guy? For sure, there were lots of weird dudes roaming Amsterdam, many of whom I'd seen multiple times, but this guy was everywhere. All I knew was he first appeared when I met Emma, and kept popping up since.

After waiting for what seemed like an eternity, the train arrived and I was off. I looked back to make sure the stranger was still on the platform. I didn't see him anywhere.

Worried he had made his way onto the train, I found a seat next to some Dutch businessmen and focused on the book. After about 20 minutes, I saw the imposing profile of Utrecht's Dom Tower. I remembered climbing it months ago. Little did I know I was looking out over Emma's home, and would soon be returning.

Once in Utrecht I transferred to Houten, your ordinary nondescript Dutch town, and called Emma. To my relief, she answered and said she'd be there soon. I paced back and forth for 15 minutes. A few times I thought I saw the mystery man. Every minute seemed like an hour, and I began to worry whether she was going to show. Maybe she had a change of heart. Anything was possible. Finally, in the distance, I saw the silhouette of a girl. It was Emma. She hadn't let me down.

Chapter 21

SEEING EMMA WALK toward me made me nervous, but in a beautiful way. In just moments, she would be taking me to her home, her safe place. Without even saying hello, she announced, "We need to go shopping." She then took my hand in hers, and we made our way to the grocery store.

There were so many times I had wished Emma was an ordinary girl, and we could do ordinary things. Now, we were doing them. She grabbed six eggs, two loaves of bread, and some Parmesan cheese. When I offered to pay, she said, "Don't make me angry." With the exception of the flowers, necklace, book, shirt, and our first dinner, she never accepted anything from me. That was the way things had to be. Our relationship was different from the start.

As we walked around the market, it was almost as if Emma was in disguise. On the outside, we looked like a normal couple, happy and thriving. On the inside, I couldn't believe I was shopping for eggs and cheese with a Dutch prostitute. Emma seemed comfortable having me around, but I could tell she was anxious too.

I carried the groceries as we took the short walk to her home. We talked mostly about what the New Year would bring. We passed schools, children, and canals. It was a traditional residential neighborhood.

Emma's apartment was on the first floor of a two-story building. It was a nice one-bedroom with wood floors and a huge television, and overlooked a park. A goldfish floated in a murky tank. Nothing hung on the walls, except for two prints of Michelangelo's Sistine Chapel and a few pictures of dogs.

We took off our shoes and Emma slid into a pair of dog-shaped slippers waiting by the door. As I sat on the couch, she disappeared into her bedroom. When she returned, she was wearing a red and black striped sweater with the word "Arrested" across the front. She said it was a gift from her brother. She tied her hair in a bun, sat on her recliner, and lit a cigarette.

"I'm glad you're here," she said warmly.

"Me too," I replied.

"Hungry?" she asked.

"Sure," I said, as she made her way into the kitchen. Emma cooked up the eggs and toast, and made a fresh pot of coffee. The scene was something out of a Norman Rockwell painting, or perhaps a Vermeer. When I offered to help, she snapped, saying no one was allowed in her kitchen. We ate mostly in silence, enjoying each other's company and the quiet around us, anticipating what was about to unfold.

Just as we finished breakfast, I heard someone approaching outside. The person seemed to be wearing sandals, which made a flip flopping sound. It sounded like leather whips against concrete. The sound was familiar, but I couldn't place it. Then, I heard aggressive knocking. The first thing that crossed my mind was . . . fuck! The creepy mystery man was making his move. I had been set up, or maybe tracked down. Either way, it didn't matter. The guy was her ex-boyfriend after all. My moment of reckoning had arrived.

A sickening feeling overcame me. How could Emma do this? How did I not see it coming? It seemed like too much of a coincidence. I was right. He had seen me spend time with her, for free, and was keeping tabs. Now, by coming to her home, I had crossed the line. Maybe this was why Emma never brought anyone home—bad things would happen.

I remembered Oliver's warning. I was in danger. Worse yet, no one knew where I was. Oliver knew the name of the town. That was all. I was off the grid. My heart pounded as I looked for an escape. I surveyed my options. As Emma went for the door, I entered panic mode.

To my surprise, I heard the voice of a girl. It wasn't the mystery man after all, but Emma's friend Sophie. She had stopped by for a visit. Sophie said hello and that she'd heard a lot about me. She then burst into a conversation with Emma that jumped back and forth between English and Dutch. Sophie had just gotten engaged to her Tunisian boyfriend. She said she was in love. Emma mostly just sat there. She then handed Sophie a stack of cash, and they gave each other a hug.

After Sophie left, Emma looked at me and said, "So, shall we begin?"

Remarkably, in that moment, I wasn't sure. Part of me was afraid to start. I had idealized Emma for so long. I liked the way things were in my mind. She was sympathetic and had a good heart. I wondered if my feelings would change once I learned the truth, and if her feelings toward me would change as well. What might I discover about the district, and what might Emma discover about herself? All I knew was I was about to go deep into her world. I took a sip of coffee, spread out on the couch, and began. It was time to learn the truth.

"Let's do it," I said.

"Great," she replied, "but one thing first."

Emma had a condition before proceeding. It was a deal breaker. She made me promise to agree, without telling me what it was. She trusted me, she said. Now I needed to trust her. My mind raced with possibilities. I agreed, and only then did she disclose the terms. At some point during the afternoon, we would have to stop and watch her favorite show. She wouldn't tell me what it was. That was a surprise. She said she never missed it, at least when she wasn't working.

With that, and a deep breath, I asked, "Everyone has a first memory. What's yours?"

Emma seemed surprised by the question. I was already getting personal. She looked down, and began.

"I was five. My mom was away all day. When she came home, my dad looked at me and said, 'I'm going to the movies.' Then, he picked me up and said, 'Whatever happens, I'll always love you.' I said, 'Please, let me come with you.' He said, 'No, it's too late. You can't come. Go to bed.' With that, he left, and he never came back."

She paused, and then laughed, "So it must have been a damn good movie."

Searching her memories, she continued, "I hated him when he left. But that was it. I grew up with no dad. I remember when we celebrated Father's Day at school for the first time. All the kids were making things for their dads. I thought, oh shit, mine's gone. I still made Father's Day things, but when I took them home, I threw them away. They didn't even reach the house."

"What role did your mom play in your life?" I asked.

"I wouldn't know. I really wouldn't know," she responded.

"Do you love her?" I asked.

"No. If anything would happen to my mom, I would have a hard time, but I can't say I love her. Too much has happened for that."

"Let's return to your dad. Did you see him after he left?" I asked.

"Only once. I turned sixteen and was starting to have problems. My mom remarried, and I didn't like my stepdad. He was an alcoholic. I started missing my dad. I begged my mom to help me find him. She knew he was in England, but that's it. She called a few people. We found him. But when I went to England to see him, it didn't work out. After I'd been there a few days, for no reason, his wife woke me up in the middle of the night and said, 'Listen, I want you out of my house.' So, there I was, at two o'clock in the morning. My dad came downstairs. I said, 'You're my father. What do you want me to do?' He said, 'My wife says she wants you out of the house, so you have to go.' Just like that. At that moment, all I could think was, you call yourself a dad?"

Already, after only a few questions, there was so much sadness. We still had a long way to go. The harsh reality of how hard this was going to be sunk in. I was going to take Emma to places she didn't want to go, and make her think about things she would rather not. She was going to have to be strong.

Hoping to change the tone, I asked, "Did you have any memorable birthdays growing up?"

"I turned eighteen and didn't see anything special," she said with a laugh. "I turned twenty-one, and there was nothing special."

"How was your relationship with your brother?" I asked.

"Do you really have to ask? We definitely did not get along. My brother is four years older, and a pain in the ass. I remember us playing outside when I was young, doing boys' things, like skateboarding, and ringing doorbells and running away. I liked playing with his trucks. He would have a truck, and I would have a truck, and we would bash them. You know, see which was stronger.

"I had a purple bike, kind of like yours," she said, laughing. "There was a bump on the street where we lived. I remember seeing my brother doing wheelies over it. I wanted to try. So, I was pedaling on my bike, doing wheel-ies, and suddenly there I was, on the ground. I was hurt and bleeding. My brother just stood there smiling. He said, 'See, you can't do things I do.' We got into an argument. He got so mad he smacked me, and called me a disgusting whore. No one had ever called me that before. Of course, that was long before I became one."

"Was that the first time anyone hit you?" I asked.

"No. I was six years old. We had a big fish tank. One night when my parents weren't home, I noticed four guilders on the tank. I knew my brother fancied some chocolate. I took the money for him, and said, 'Come on, let's get you some candy.' I was trying to be a good sister. A few days later, my stepdad asked, 'Where's that money gone?' I didn't remember taking it, because normally I don't steal. It wasn't even for me. I've never stolen from my parents, so I didn't remember. He got mad and hit me so hard, again and again, that my ass was really blue—all for four guilders. The guy was huge, always drunk, and had big hands, farmer hands. The bruise was so bad we had to put disinfectant all over it. My brother had ratted me out."

"Did things change for the better when your mom got divorced?" I asked.

"When my stepdad left, I thought, good, now I've got time with my mom. I imagined us going to the city, doing mother and daughter stuff. That didn't happen. She was away most of the time. I saw her once a week, if I was lucky. Then my mom found a new guy. The guy and I hated each other because I wanted to spend time with my mom. I thought, I see my mom maybe once a week. You see her every day. I'm her daughter, and what are you? You're just a guy. I always said to my mom, 'I'm your daughter, don't forget that. Guys come and go.' My mom didn't care."

"Were there any moments you felt loved?" I asked.

She paused and searched her memories. "No. Never."

"Well," I continued, trying to make her smile, "what was the best thing your mom ever did for you?"

"She made me corned beef hash," she said apathetically.

"Can you describe her? What are her interests?"

"Men. My mom wants to have her second youth. I mean, she was eighteen when she had her first child. I don't have a good relationship with her. Usually, when we talk, it goes like this: 'Hi, how are you?' 'I'm fine, how are you?' 'Fine.' 'What are you doing?' 'Nothing. What are you doing?' 'Yeah, I'm doing nothing.' 'OK.' 'I'll call you next week.' 'Bye.' 'Bye.' I can talk to my mom for maybe ten minutes, and then not speak with her for a month or two. It's normal. She's not interesting."

"What are her values?" I asked.

"She doesn't have any."

Hoping to bring her back to a period of innocence, I asked, "Who were you in school? What was your scene?"

"I was the girl with pigtails, long dark hair, and stupid clothes. I mean, there were girls who had parents with good jobs, who lived in big houses, and who wore nice clothes. I had clothes my mom made. People would say, 'What have you got on? Did your mom make those from curtains?' They would laugh. When I heard that kind of stuff, I would just go away. I would leave school and come home, crying. I had to change schools, again and again.

"That all changed at my last school. I was sixteen and became a big boss, always starting fights and getting in trouble. I had jeans with rips in them. Everyone would write on them. I wore sneakers, baggy sweaters, and a baseball cap. Usually my hair was in a ponytail. I had very long hair. I never wore makeup. I was like a guy. There was nothing feminine about me. When guys from school see me now, looking all sexy and appealing, they say, 'My God, Emma, what happened to you!'"

"What were your favorite and least favorite subjects?" I asked.

"History was something I liked, but I hated arithmetic," Emma said, giving it some thought. "Actually, I hated everything about school. Homework, what's that? I usually said to my mom, 'No, I don't have any homework. I did it all.' I didn't like school, so I didn't do any work."

"Did anything good ever happen at school?" I asked, thinking her memories couldn't all be bad.

"Yeah, once. I was having a real shit day. I just started school in Utrecht. It was a twenty minute bike ride from my town. It was pissing down rain. I came to school soaking wet, and had Dutch lessons. This girl looks at me and says, 'God, she's having one of those days again.' I said, 'Shut your face. Don't talk to me.' She said, 'Oh, see! She's having one of those days.' I stood up and smacked her one. I was sent to the principal and got suspended. I went home, put down my things, and went out. That was the best thing that happened. Getting suspended. Growing up, I didn't think about sex. I didn't think about guys. The only thing I thought about was how to save my ass, and get money."

"When was your first kiss? Everyone has one," I asked, wanting to give her a hug.

"I was fourteen," she said. "I was taking karate three times a week. On Saturdays, there was a guy, and I kind of liked him. He was seventeen. One day he asked me out. I said fine. We went to the movies. At the end of the date, we stood for a moment in front of my flat. He said, 'How about a kiss?' I gave him a quick kiss and said bye. He said, 'No, give me a good kiss.' I thought, what does that even mean? There I was, not knowing what to do. I kissed him again and ran off. That was my first kiss. After that, I didn't go to karate anymore. I was finished."

"What was your group of friends like back then?" I asked.

"They were all the same. They were bad news, really bad people. But what the hell, everything was better than going home. We got into trouble. We got into stealing. It would always be shitty things not even worth stealing. I would steal candy, puddings, and makeup. On the Mercedes Benz, they have the emblem, right? We would take it off and put it on our necklaces—the bigger the better. That kind of thing.

"One day, I went with a friend to a drugstore. We both had money on us. She started putting on makeup, and then I saw her stealing some. I thought, I want a pencil, so I'll take one as well. You know, shitty things. As I was walking out, the police came for us. They saw her pinching the eye shadow. It was her fault we got snatched.

"Another time, we thought this person was on vacation. Two of our guy friends did a stakeout, and my girlfriend and I went into his house. Just for fun. We went in, looked around, and went directly to the refrigerator. We took some things to eat and drink. That's all. Then, all of a sudden, I saw a huge man in his underwear standing in front of us. He said, 'Excuse me, what are you doing?' I said, 'I'm looking for the toilet.' Yeah, right! So we got caught. Meanwhile, our guy friends saw the lights go on and split. Assholes. The man called the police but didn't press charges."

Emma then asked, "What's up with all these questions about my childhood? Who am I? I'm not interesting," she said sadly. "No one's going to care about this stuff."

"You're wrong, Emma," I said. "You matter. Your story matters."

"Yeah, right," she said, as she stood up from her recliner and slid next to me on the couch. At that moment, I couldn't help but think what would happen if I tried to kiss her. How would she respond? Was she expecting it, or would it ruin everything?

"So, that's it? All done with your questions?" she asked.

"Nah, I have a few more," I said.

"Good. What's next?"

I gave her a warm smile, taking everything in, and continued.

Chapter 22

"HERE'S A QUESTION," I said, as Emma inched closer on the couch. "When you were little, what did you want to be when you grew up?"

Emma thought about it for a second. It was apparently something that hadn't crossed her mind in a while. Finally, she said, "My mom had a friend. She was a stewardess. I spent a lot of time with her. That was the first thing I wanted to be. But, as you know, I never became one."

"What was your first job?"

"My mom's boyfriend had a music shop. I sold CDs. I cleaned up. I helped customers. I left because of my mom. Eventually, she wanted to work there too. I wasn't about to work with her. Not after everything she'd done. So, I got another job in a magazine shop. But then the owner broke up with his girlfriend, and said, 'I don't want you working here anymore. You remind me of my ex. You have to go.'"

"And then?" I asked.

"I had so many jobs. The next was a clothing store in Utrecht, but the tax department came and closed it down."

"Did you ever have a job you liked?" I asked, amazed at her bad luck.

"Once. I worked with kids, older people, and women who wanted to get back on their feet. I would interview them, get them into school, and get them jobs. Imagine that. I liked the responsibility. I gave orders to eight men. That felt great, but I got sick and my contract ended."

"Growing up, were there certain things you said you would never do?" I asked, still reflecting on her job history, and thinking the world had literally conspired against her.

"Only one," she said, sadly. "I would always tell my mom I would never become a prostitute. Never. How low can you go? Amazing, huh? Look at me now."

"When did you first consider becoming one?" I asked.

"The day my stepdad threw me out," Emma said, expressionless. "I used to always carry a knife. One day, he said to me, 'I don't want your knife in my house.' I said, 'I need it for protection.' That was the truth. He said, 'OK, you can choose. Throw the knife away, or leave this house.' I said, 'Fine, I'm leaving.' I got my stuff and left. My boyfriend picked me up. We talked. He said, 'I know something we can do, but I need your honest opinion. I need money. You need money. It's the only solution.' I went to Arnhem, and that's when it started. I began working as a prostitute. I was nineteen.

"Looking back, I think it was more his idea than mine," she continued. "Yeah, definitely. I just thought, I've been with him for a while, so let's do it. Good opportunity, right? At the moment, I didn't have a roof over my head, and I had no money. That's why I went."

"What else was going on in your mind?" I asked.

"You hear stories. You hear about lots of money. You think, fine, I'll do it for five months, maybe six. I'll get my own car, my own house, and have money. You think it's the fast life. You don't see the shit you take with you. You think it's easy. Just lie there, open your legs, and say next."

"What was the first day like?"

"When you walk through the district, you see girls and lights. The first thing that comes to mind is, that's easy money. But, from the moment you stand behind the glass, and see what you have to do, it's hell. I can't describe it actually. You feel cheap and disgusting. It's like going to the butcher. You feel like that. I mean, you walk into the butcher shop and say you want a schnitzel or whatever. It's the same in the district. You feel like a piece of meat.

"After I finished my first day, I went directly to my boy-friend. The only thing he asked was, 'How much money did we make?' The first day I made eight hundred guilders. You see the money, and think, this is easy! Then, on the second day, you think, what am I doing here? On the third, you feel disgusting, and so on. You feel cheaper and cheaper, every day, for as long as you are there, until there's just about nothing left."

"Did you talk to other girls before starting?" I asked. "Anyone give you lessons?"

"No, not really. There aren't lessons," Emma said. "It's nature. With time, you learn. It's just like life. You get better. On my first day, my boyfriend picked up one of his friends. She was also a prostitute. It was my first time meeting her.

We spoke for ten minutes. She told me a few things, like don't lie like a dead person. Make noise. That turns men on. If the guy only wants a blowjob, try to get a fuck out of it. I learned how to talk to customers, and the things you can't do, like kissing and all that shit. The only thing you can do is give blowjobs, give hand jobs, and get laid. That's it. The rest is not allowed because of disease."

"How did you get a window?" I asked.

"My boyfriend asked his friend. It was easy. I just went to this guy, paid him money, and that was that. Nothing else was required, as long as I paid rent. The only thing he asked was how old I was. You aren't allowed to work until eighteen. I was nineteen, so no problem."

"What were you most afraid of?" I asked.

"How do I get a guy inside? How do I earn money? What happens if he doesn't cum, and makes trouble? Maybe he'll beat me up, you never know. Those were the things I thought about. Nothing else. The first location had three windows that shared a door. There was a girl next to me who was always dancing, feeling good. She wore almost nothing. I had a white dress on because I didn't want to stand in my underwear. She was smiling at guys, saying, 'Come on, it's only fifty guilders.' She said to me, 'Go on, dance.' So I moved a bit, and danced. All I could think was, I want to go home. Please, please, let me go home.

"Then a guy came to my window. He could tell I was new. There are lots of guys who need to try out every new girl. He seemed to be one of them. When he came to the door, I thought, God, please help me. Save me from this place. He just said, 'I'm coming in.' I let him in and said, 'Listen, this is my first day. I might be a bit clumsy.' We started talking. Usually they make you feel at ease, instead of the other way around."

"Do you remember what he looked like?" I asked.

"No. It's a total blank. I wanted it over with as soon as possible. When they leave, they leave. You don't think about them anymore. It's all about money. It's not a person. It's a walking bank."

"Was there anything fun about it?"

"No, absolutely not. It wasn't a kick. It wasn't a thrill. It was money, pure money. I mean, you're selling your body. There is nothing fun about that. Any girl who tells you different is lying or crazy."

"Nothing made you feel good? Not even the attention?" I asked.

"No. You don't have emotions. It's not like you care what kind of men are outside. I'm not standing behind a window to get laid by a good-looking guy. You can go to a disco for that. It was a total nightmare, from the day I started, and still is."

I listened as Emma talked about her experiences with poise and reflection. She had no agenda other than to share her feelings, and her words spilled out with rawness and resolve. Her life was even worse than I imagined. Surprisingly, though, the more I learned about her, the more my feelings grew.

"What happened to your relationship with your boyfriend after you started?" I asked.

"After seven months, we had a fight. I was sick of the routine of him beating me up, going back to work, coming home, getting beaten up, giving him all my money, getting beaten up again, leaving him, going back to my mom, going back to him, and then getting beaten up all over again. I went into the bedroom, packed my things, and left. There I was, at midnight, with two plastic bags, and nowhere to call home."

"What started the fight?" I asked.

"It was a Thursday I'll never forget. I was standing in my window and took an ecstasy pill. All of a sudden, one of the prostitutes asked, 'What's wrong with you?' I said, 'I don't know. I'm getting kind of nervous. Maybe it's the pill, but I think my boyfriend is screwing my best friend.' She started laughing. 'You're going nuts! You're losing it. You shouldn't take any more pills.' I said, 'No, really. I have a weird feeling in my stomach. I think my boyfriend is sleeping with another girl.' She said, 'Why don't you call him then?' I called. He didn't answer. I thought I could do one of two things. I could stay in my window and wait for him to pick me up, or I could go home and try to catch him. I went home.

"When I walked in, he was alone, but I noticed two glasses on the counter. When I asked who had been over, he said a guy friend. I didn't believe him. I went to the bathroom. He had taken a shower. 'You never shower when I'm not here,' I said. 'You wait.' He yelled, 'I came home and wanted one. What's your problem?' Also, that day when I made the bed, I turned a corner of the sheets over. I had never done that before, but I did that morning. The bed had been used. He said he was sleeping. I said, 'When you come home from work, you lie on the couch. You never go to bed.' From that moment on, I knew.

"A few weeks later, something inside me said I had to read my best friend's diary. I'm not the kind of person who does that kind of thing. Given the circumstances, I started reading. It was all there. The day I had the feeling was the day he screwed my best friend, and he screwed her in my bed. I had been betrayed.

"At first, I didn't know what to do. I was afraid of confronting him. One night, the three of us were watching television. I had been working all day and went to bed. I started dreaming he was kissing her. I woke up and didn't see him next to me. I figured he had fallen asleep in the living room. I got out of bed, went to the living room, and there they were. She was naked, and they were kissing.

"I didn't say a thing. I just went mad. I went into the bedroom and started throwing things. I then went into the living room, pulled the blanket off my best friend, and yelled, 'I'm not finished with you.' My boyfriend screamed, 'Leave her alone!' I went into the kitchen. I got the biggest knife I could find. I looked at her, I looked at him, and everything went blank. I just started stabbing. He grabbed a cushion from the couch, and I stabbed it, over and over. Feathers flew everywhere. He then hit me so hard I blanked out. That was the craziest I ever got. Believe me, if I had the chance to do it again, I would. Next time, I say leave the pillow behind, please. That was my last serious boyfriend. I lost him and my best friend the same day."

Holy shit, I thought. "Did you ever love the guy?" I asked.

"I don't think I know the meaning of love, because I've never had it," she said softly. "Maybe someday, though." Emma slid off her slippers and kicked her legs up on my lap. "Mind giving me a foot massage?" she asked. "I stand all day you know."

Gently massaging her feet, I asked, "After you broke up, where did you live? Where did you go that night?"

"I didn't go anywhere," she said emotionlessly. "I went back to my window and stayed there. I worked there. I slept there. I ate there. For the next two years, I was in my window, eating, sleeping, and fucking. The bed where I worked was the bed where I slept. A guy would deliver food. There I was, twenty-four hours a day, for two years straight."

Hearing all this saddened me beyond belief. Going in, I knew I would learn things impossible to imagine, but this was too much. For two straight years, Emma was in a window. The thought was inconceivable. It was almost as if once she entered the world of prostitution, she was afraid to leave. In her mind, she no longer felt welcome anywhere else.

Still massaging her toes, I asked, "What did your mom think? What did you tell her?"

Emma scowled, tired of the questions about her mother. "At first, I didn't tell her anything. It's my business, not hers. One day, her new boyfriend said, 'If I were you, I'd go to Arnhem and see what your daughter is doing.' When my mom asked me about it, I said I was there for a cleaning job. A few days later, I started having a good day. The weather was warm, and I had earned a lot. I was talking to one of the girls, laughing. Suddenly, I turned my head and there he was. My mom's boyfriend was standing right in front of me, smiling.

"It was the most embarrassing moment. I called my mom a few days later and asked why she sent him. She coldly replied, 'He went by himself.' I said, 'I know why. So he can have you to himself. He's hoping you don't ever want to see me again.' I then told my mom what she wanted to hear. I said, 'You don't have a daughter anymore. She's finished.' I hung up the phone, and there I was."

"And then?" I ask. "When did you speak with her next?"

"Three months later," Emma said. "I called because I needed help. My dog was dying. From that moment on, we started talking again."

"What did she say about you working?"

"She didn't say anything because we were too busy with the dog. I had my own life. I didn't live in her house anymore."

"She didn't tell you to stop?"

"No, not in the beginning. She finally did a few months ago. I was sick of lying to everybody about what I was doing. I called her, and said, 'Listen, I'm in Amsterdam and working again.' She said, 'You don't have to work. You have a good life. I don't like knowing my daughter is a prostitute.' I said, 'This is my life, not yours. I pay my bills.'"

Emotionally exhausted, Emma needed a break. I needed one too. Also, her sweater was itching and she needed to put on something more comfortable. She stood up, made herself a cup of coffee, and went into the bedroom to change. I sat on the couch and waited for her to return. After a few minutes, I went to find her. She had changed into sweats and a tank top, and was lying face up on her bed.

"Sorry," she said, "it's hard talking about all this. I need a few minutes. Come lie with me." I lay down on her bed, and Emma put her hand on my chest. We then just lay there, breathing the same air, in a state of suspension. The moment was intimate, and had nothing to do with sex. We seemed to be developing a relationship based on something far deeper.

Chapter 23

WE EVENTUALLY MADE our way back to the living room, ready for more questions and answers. "When was the first time you tried drugs?" I asked, wasting no time.

"When I was in school, during the day, we went to shopping malls. At night, we went to a playground. I was fifteen. One night, a friend of mine was rolling a joint. I asked, 'What's that?' He said, 'It's a joint. Do you want a drag?' I took a hit. At first, I felt weird. Then I started laughing, and felt great. That was the first time."

"Did you smoke a lot after that?" I asked.

"No, not every day. Sometimes at parties, or when I felt shitty, but that's it." Like so many Dutch, Emma could care less about cannabis.

"What did you experiment with next?" I asked.

"I started with cocaine," Emma replied. "I was working in my window. I wanted to go home but hadn't made enough money. I was tired. My boyfriend said, 'You stay in there.' I cried, 'No, please. I need to go home. I can't do this anymore today.' He glared at me and said, 'You stay in there because you didn't earn enough money.' I was pissed. A girl said, 'Let's go upstairs and do a line.' I had never touched the stuff before. I saw her pouring cocaine into a cigarette. I asked, 'What are you doing? What does it do to you?' She smiled and said, 'It makes you feel really good, and you stop thinking about things.' Just like that, I started smoking cocaine. I liked it. I started using it so regularly I lost weight, and I started crying over stupid things.

"A year later ecstasy was everywhere. One day, after a fight with my boyfriend, I tried it. It was great. When he found out, he said, 'Let's go for a walk.' He then took me into a vegetable garden and beat the shit out of me. I thought I was going to die. I really thought it was my last day. For a while after that, I kept taking the pills. One day my mom said, 'You look like a bloody ghost.' I looked in the mirror, and I did—I looked like a ghost. I stopped the pills, and didn't touch anything for a while.

"That was until I started up with cocaine again a few weeks ago. I was feeling shitty. I didn't earn diddly. Another girl had some, made a line, and asked if I wanted some. Actually, the day you came behind my window was the first time I used again. I won't use it now, you know, in normal life. When I'm working, it's different. You're in another world. You think, what the hell. Without drugs, you stand there and think, what am I doing here? Please get me out of here. If you use drugs, you don't give a shit what people think, or how people look at you, or whether they come inside. You just think, go on. Are you finished? Thank you.

Bye. Have a nice day. Thanks for the money, idiot. You stand, you dance, you smile, you feel good, and then you forget."

"How did you end up working in Amsterdam?" I asked.

"Arnhem is a small Dutch town. Amsterdam is Amsterdam. I went for the money. At first, you go from window to window. When you start, you don't have the same room every time. It keeps getting rented. All of a sudden, you come into a place and say, 'Hey, this is good. I want to stay here.' You tell them, 'If this room is ever available, I want it, day or night, every day.'"

"Who owns the windows?" I asked.

"You don't usually know who owns them. I know the boss who owns mine on Bethlemsteeg because he walks around a lot. In other windows you never see the owners. They are guys in the underworld. They don't just own windows. They do all kinds of bad shit. You don't have any contact with them, unless they ask you out. They have boys walking around picking up the rent."

"How does rent work?"

"You pay daily," she said. "In Amsterdam, you pay two hundred guilders from noon until eight. The same for the second shift, which lasts from eight onwards."

"Do girls lose money?"

"There are some girls who don't earn anything," she said.

"What rules are there in the De Wallen?" I continued.

"You have to be at least eighteen years old, and have to carry your passport in case the police check. Inside, you are allowed to work from fifty guilders and up. That's fifty guilders for a blowjob or screw, and one hundred guilders for both. If you say fifty guilders for a blowjob and a fuck, you are out. You can forget it. That's a strict rule for all the windows near the church. In some windows far away, you can ask whatever you want."

"How would anyone find out?" I asked.

"Customers talk. If you come to me and I say, 'OK, sweetie, fifty guilders for a blowjob and a fuck,' you might tell your friends. They might tell their friends, and girls hear. You could go to my neighbor next time and say, 'Oh, well, the girl next door does it all for fifty.' That's the way it works."

When the euro replaced the guilder, and the price of everything doubled overnight, it became fifty euros for a fuck and a suck. But not yet. Not in 1999.

"What's your relationship like with the other girls?" I asked.

"I generally don't talk to them. Why should I? Am I there to socialize? No. I'm there to make money. If I want friends, I have them outside the streets."

"Girls seem strict about the fifteen minutes. Is that a rule too?" I asked.

"It's been that way since long before I was born. That's not a rule. That's tradition."

"What's your daily routine?" I asked.

"Really?" she replied, laughing. "My routine is getting laid all day. Giving blowjobs all day. Standing in my window and waiting for the next customer. Every day we go to Lunch Room 52 to get toilet paper. You know, for condoms and to wipe off our hands when we use jelly. Otherwise, beneath you will be a pile of condoms with sperm in them. That's not really nice, not at all. You take the condoms off with toilet paper and throw them out. That's the routine."

"Do you get tired standing?"

"Yeah," she said. "It's exhausting."

"Do you listen to the men outside?"

"You can," she said. "You hear things like, 'Wow, look at her,' and, 'Please, can I come in for free?' Those kinds of things. 'Man, I wouldn't screw her if she was the last woman on Earth.' Actually, you hear everything," she said sadly.

Still searching for something positive, I asked, "Do you ever have good days? Are you ever happy?"

"No," she said, almost reflexively. "How can you be happy if you have to sell your body? That's why I sometimes use drugs, to look happy."

"The other girls generally feel the same?"

"I'm pretty sure they do, but some aren't as quick to admit it. It's one big show, unless you're a nymphomaniac. There are a few of those, but not many."

"How many years have you worked?" I asked.

"Five," she said.

"How many guys would you estimate you've been with?"

"I don't know. I can't guess. It would be impossible."

"On an average day, how many?" I asked.

"I can't say. On one day, it could be so busy, one after another, but I only make six hundred guilders. On another day, I've only got five customers, but I make two thousand."

"Do you ever wear perfume?" I asked, never having noticed her wear any.

"No. If a guy comes in who is married, and we get lots of those, you will get perfume on him. His clothes will smell. His body will smell. Most guys don't want that."

"Do you have issues sleeping with married men?"

"No, I get them all the time. They pay. I think it's good we're here. If we weren't, they would go elsewhere and commit adultery. Maybe get a girl pregnant, and destroy their marriage."

"How do you feel about your body when in a window?" I asked.

"Fat and ugly," she said, laughing, which was hard to believe. "What woman doesn't? I think every woman feels that way. When you see women with long blond hair and big tits, you feel worse. You see girls with silicone breasts. Before they get them, they don't earn diddly. Then they earn like crazy. It's unbelievable, and it's true. I've seen it with my own eyes. Many girls only wear thongs, but I can't stand in my underwear. I usually have something else on. Otherwise I don't feel right."

"Have friends ever randomly found you?" I asked.

"Yes. Loads of times friends walk by and see me. The first couple times you think, shit. But then you think, what the hell? It's my life, not yours. If you don't like me because I'm a prostitute, then, well, piss off. I don't need you. They ask, 'What are you doing here?' I say, 'Working.' They say, 'I see that, but why?' I say, 'It's none of your business. You see me here, and that's enough. You don't need to know more.'"

"Where do you eat when working in Amsterdam?" I asked.

"I barely eat. If I eat, it's a good day and I cook for myself. Otherwise, I can go two days, perhaps three, without eating. Why? I don't know. You get used to it. When you are in prostitution, the time you're eating, you could be with customers. That means you could go home earlier. Why should I stay here, and eat, when I could be home at ten? So I think, I'll eat later. But then, when I get home, I take a shower and just go to bed. If I don't eat, I don't care."

Chapter 24

WE HAD BEEN talking for a while now, but since our last break Emma showed no signs of tiring. If anything, she seemed to be gaining in strength with every question. Knowing it was my last day in Holland, and maybe the last time I would ever see Emma, I tried to take in as much as possible. What amazed me most was that Emma was letting down her guard. It was like one long therapy session, long overdue. I felt closer to her than ever. I could tell she felt close to me too.

"You mentioned you never received lessons," I continued. "What are some things you've learned after all these years? Any tricks?" I asked.

"When a customer pays before we begin, I look in his wallet. If I see money, I have a trick. I make the guy so horny until he's about to cum, and then say, 'Sorry, time's up! What do you want to do? Do you want to go further, or do you want to stop?' Most guys want to go further. They want to finish. So they pay more. But they can't just keep going. They have to stop, get up, grab their wallet, and pay me first.

It's not as if I say, 'You can pay more later. Stay and finish.' No way. I say, 'Get up. Get the money.' So we have to start all over again. Then, again, when they're just about to cum, I say, 'Sorry, time's up! Are you going to pay me, or am I going to stop?' The guy is usually so horny he'll pay. That's the trick. It's really the only one I use. Also, usually, it's twenty-five guilders extra to take off my bra."

She paused, thought a bit, and continued. "A few months ago, I had a threesome with a German girl. The customer was English. He paid me, and he paid her. The girl then said to me, 'Keep your clothes on.' So I kept my clothes on. Then, when she went to give him a blowjob, she really wasn't doing anything. German girls use their hands, and just make the movements. I thought, my God, how does she get away with that? When she went to have sex with him, she climbed on top. She put it between her backside, held it in her hand, and gripped it nice and tight. It was as if it was going in, but it wasn't. This was just amazing. She was getting paid to do nothing, really nothing, just scream and moan. That's something I'd never seen before. I heard about it. German girls are known for it. That was the first time I saw it. Now, I do that with Chinese people, because it's so tiny and they haven't invented a condom small enough. I mean, we are talking the size of my pinky finger. When I put a condom on, they nearly swim in it."

"What are your rules?" I asked.

"No kissing my neck, no kissing my breasts, no kissing anything, and no feeling around because of infections. No fingering or anything like that. Positions are allowed if you pay for them, but not all. No anal. No ninety-six."

"You mean sixty-nine?"

"Yeah, sixty-nine," she said, laughing. "For us, it's the same thing. There are people who ask for sex without a condom, or ask, 'Can I lick you?' Those kinds of things I don't do. You can't come in with a buddy, or as a couple with your girlfriend or wife. I don't do that. Some girls do. I have limits. I don't like people beating me up—definitely not. I've had enough of that."

"Does sex ever hurt?" I asked.

"We use lots of jelly. You don't feel a thing."

"What's your average customer like?" I asked. "Is there a certain kind of guy who comes to you?"

"Everything comes in. I get guys in T-shirts and also fancy suits. I get lots of Turkish guys, dark guys, and Dutch and English guys. Americans too," she said. "I get dentists, doctors, and lots of lawyers. Once, when working outside Amsterdam, I had a big-time Hollywood director. He came in at eight in the evening and wanted sadomasochism. Humiliation and all that shit. I had a big room with two doors. If you opened the back door, you were in a garden. Behind the garden were train tracks. It was pouring rain and freezing cold. The director said he wanted to be humiliated, so I told him to take off his clothes. I took him outside, naked. I tied him up and made him stand on a brick in the garden, facing the tracks. I then went inside and carried on with other customers. As if that wasn't enough, after each customer, I would go outside and beat him up. This lasted until seven the next morning. For eleven hours, he was outside, naked, on a brick, in the freezing rain, getting beaten up over and over, with passenger trains rolling by, one after another, every half hour. He was looking like a real ass. He paid good money for this! To top it off, he paid another girl to pee on him. That's what you get with famous people. They often just want to be humiliated."

She continued, "I have an American who likes me to spank him and talk dirty. That's all. He pays two hundred guilders and stays fifteen minutes. I get lots of sickos, really. You get all kinds of people. Some want to dress up like little girls and wear lipstick. Of course, you get people who come for a blowjob, or a massage, and then leave, or people who only want to talk. Every day is a different day, and then you forget it.

"Sometimes, I get customers who want to take me out. One guy pays a thousand guilders and I don't have to do a thing—only go to dinner, play on his computer, and drink coffee. Once, a guy took three of us home. We stayed an hour and did nothing except drink and smoke. You don't get those often, but you get them. Sometimes, you get customers who say, 'It's not for me. I want to satisfy you.' Usually, it's a vibrator show, and they think I get off. You moan and groan, and say, 'Ah, that was great! Come back again. I can't wait until you come back again.' We are all performers."

"Do you prefer tourists or locals?" I asked.

"Tourists get drunk and high, and usually pay better, but they can be a pain in the ass. Locals know the rules. With foreigners, you have to tell them over and over, 'Don't touch me here, don't touch me there,' and, 'You have to pay extra for this, you have to pay extra for that.'"

"Have you ever been frightened by a customer?" I continued.

"Never, but there are arguments. Chinese people and I do not get along. Absolutely not. Every time a Chinese guy wants to come in, I know there's going to be trouble. When they pay, they think they can touch you everywhere. Kiss you. Do whatever. I usually end up calling security."

"What's your relationship like with the police?"

"We don't have one. They come in, check our age, and that's it."

"Do you feel safe?"

"We have an alarm system. If there's a problem, I pull the string, the same string you were playing with. Security comes in seconds. I call them when dealing with drunken people, and Chinese guys. I say, 'Time's up,' and they don't want to go. I say, 'Listen, you have to go, or you have to pay more.' They say, 'No, I'm staying here. I haven't cum yet.' I say, 'I don't give a shit. Pay more then.' At that point, I say, 'You have two choices: you can get dressed, or I can call security. Your choice.' When they still don't leave, I call. Security listens to both sides, and then asks the guy to leave. If he doesn't, he gets thrown out. But I certainly don't feel in control. Absolutely not. He's the paying customer. He says what's happening, not me. Once he puts money down, he's the one in control. He paid for a blowjob, so I'd better give him one."

"Does it matter if they're gross?"

"You close your eyes, just like normal sex. If it's good, you close your eyes. You don't have to look, but you do feel them breathing on you. Often, they are the best paying customers. Recently, I had one who was so fat he couldn't get it in, so I gave him a hand job. He paid three hundred guilders for fifteen minutes."

"Is body odor ever a problem?"

"If a guy smells bad, I won't let him in. No is no, and people get pissed. As long as I close the door, they don't come in. I just look the other way. I don't let junkies in. They have to be clean. I look at their hands, nails, and the way they dress."

"What's the youngest you've been with?" I asked.

"They have to be at least eighteen," Emma replied. "Just like us. Once, I had a little boy come over. I thought the kid was joking. He looked fourteen. He said, 'I've got my passport.' Yeah, he was eighteen, so I let him in. If cops saw this kid walk out my door, and he didn't have a passport, I would've had a problem."

"The oldest?"

"He was eighty-five. You don't have sex with these people, because they can't. It's more about you just being there. It's about lying next to them, and talking. That's it. I won't have sex with a guy who is eighty-five. I might give him a heart attack or something."

"Do many guys have performance issues?"

"Yes. A lot. Usually it's nerves, especially when they've never been with a prostitute. Often, they're just too drunk, high, or used too much coke. They're easy money. You can see when a person is that messed up. You think, that's nice. They get so embarrassed they keep paying. Once, I had an

English guy, a pervert. He had a good drink. I kept him for an hour, and got nine hundred guilders out of him. He liked me to scratch his back."

"Ever work in a brothel?"

"A friend of mine worked in a brothel. One day, she asked if I wanted to go. I said fine. You put on your evening dress, sit at the bar, and get drunk out of your mind. You have to get as many drinks out of customers as you can. In a brothel, guys stay for at least an hour. If you want to stay longer, that's fine, but you're not allowed to pay for less. Rooms are different than the windows. They're chicer. It's a world for rich people, not people who just want fifteen minutes. Unlike in the windows, you generally can't say no to a customer. Most kiss them, and screw them any way they want. That's not for me. I don't want any diseases. I've only been once. I'll never go back."

"What are your thoughts on legalization?" I asked.

"Even in Holland, it's not really legal. If it was, we'd all pay taxes. Girls want the money for themselves. They don't want to lie on their backs just to pay Mr. Taxman. You can't track the money a girl makes, especially in the windows. That's why it will never really be legal. But, at least in Holland, girls don't have to work on the streets. In the windows, things are safer."

"Are diseases a problem?"

"No, not really. I think most girls in the windows are like me. Health comes first. But yes, I worry. Money is nice, but I think my life is worth, maybe, more. I get checkups once a month."

"Ever have a condom break?" I asked.

"Just once, in Arnhem. I'll never forget it. It broke, and I couldn't have done anything about it. It was a fabric fault. I was worried. I went to a special place for prostitutes. They gave me a checkup, and a week later I had to come back for another. A week after that, they checked me again. I had to do AIDS tests for half a year. I was fine."

"After all these experiences, how do you see men?" I asked.

"They are dogs. They only think about sex. Since I've been working, I don't think I could trust a guy very easily. You walk around town and look at all those happily married men. But they go to prostitutes."

"Do many try to save you?"

"In any given day, it happens at least three times. They say, 'Such a smart girl, what are you doing here?' I say, money."

"Have you ever climaxed while working?"

"No. Never," Emma replied. "Not even once. They are strange men. Other than money, the only thing I think is that there is a disgusting, fat, old, stoned, or drunk stranger on top of me. Please, are the fifteen minutes up? That's the only thing going through my mind."

"Do you satisfy yourself outside work?"

"No, absolutely not. As a prostitute, you put off all your emotions. Sex is not important. If you're in the business for too long, it spoils you. It really does. You look at things in a very different way. Sex is sex. There's no feeling anymore. It sounds stupid, but it's true. If I had a boyfriend, I would say, don't expect me to think, oh, yippee, I'm having sex. Not the first time. Not the second time. Maybe in a few months, but I'd have to learn everything all over again. I'd have to learn how to feel."

Chapter 25

AFTER SEVERAL UNINTERRUPTED hours of digging into her world, the time had come to watch her show, the one I promised to watch before the interview began. We still had ground to cover, but, given the intensity of our chat, I was happy to take a break. It would be good for us both.

Emma curled up next to me and turned on the TV. I had never seen her more excited about anything. I had no idea what to expect. The show came on, and I knew it. It was *The Jerry Springer Show*. Just like *The A-Team,* it was broadcast in English with Dutch subtitles. Emma told me watching it was the only time she felt good about herself. As bad as things were in her world, in her mind the people on the show always seemed to have it worse. A few times I tried to make small talk, but Emma would have none of it. She was transfixed.

When the episode ended, Emma made her way into the kitchen to make dinner. On the menu was macaroni with homemade meat sauce, a recipe from her grandmother.

When I asked if I could help, she snapped, "I told you. No one comes into my kitchen when I cook!"

"Come on," I said, "I leave tomorrow. Some rules are meant to be broken."

She looked at me, shaking her head, and said, "Fine, but I'm doing all the cooking." I put my arms around her waist, and she didn't push me off.

The food smelled delicious, and she kept telling me she never cooked for anyone. Now, she was making an exception for the second time that day, if you count breakfast. I was her special guest. With dinner ready, I helped her set the table and took a seat.

"Aren't you forgetting something?" she asked, as she lit a candle and dimmed the lights. "Now, we can eat," she said.

During dinner, she must have asked five times if I liked her cooking. I said yes and was honest. It was a fine meal, and I was aware it would likely be our final one together, our last supper. After everything we'd been through, there we were, sharing a simple meal. It's been said the greatest moments in life are when you step out of your comfort zone. Needless to say, I had done just that, since we met. But in that moment, in her home, I felt more comfortable than ever.

"I usually don't have dinner guests," she said again. "This is nice. I'm glad you're here." During dinner, I could tell she was tired and emotionally depleted. We didn't say much, mostly just looking into each other's eyes. Once we finished, I helped with the dishes, and we sat down together on the couch. With her head leaning on my shoulder, we continued where we left off.

"Is it hard going back and forth between worlds?" I asked.

"Yeah, because as a prostitute, you're a different person. Like I said, you're a performer. You become the person the customer wants you to be. You're in a different world. When you are around other prostitutes, the outside world doesn't interest you. Not at all. The world of prostitution becomes your home. When you come back to this world, people ask, 'So, what have you been doing?' You hear people talk about prostitution, and prostitutes. You hear the names. You feel so low.

"Often, I feel like I don't want to go on. I'll sit on a ledge, ten stories high, and think, I'm going to jump. I'm really going to jump this time. That's what I want. I have tried to cut my wrists several times. I have often thought I don't want to open my eyes anymore. Because I think, is this life? Being a prostitute, over thirteen hours a day? This is not the life I want. I come home late at night. I take a shower because I feel disgusting. I get into bed, and if I'm lucky, I can sleep. Usually, I just lie there. The next day, I get up, make myself coffee, get dressed, get on the train, and by twelve o'clock, I've started again.

"Sometimes, I lock myself in the shower with all the pills I can find. I collect them from doctors. As a prostitute, you get the feeling you can't do anything right. You get the feeling you don't fit into this world, because people think, 'Prostitution is disgusting. Hookers are disgusting. Once a whore, always a whore.' Since you don't fit into this world, and since you don't matter, why not end it? That's what you think."

The thought of Emma trying to kill herself, repeatedly, was hard to take. In fact, it was heartbreaking. In that moment, there was nothing I could do but continue with my questions. But the more she opened up, the harder it was to carry on.

"If there is an afterlife, where do you think you'll go?" I asked.

"Hell," she replied, after reflecting for a moment. "After all the things I've done—prostitution, stealing, lying, drugs. Hell, definitely."

"No chance of redemption?" I asked.

"Don't think so," she said sadly. "Come back in twenty years and ask."

"Do you believe in God?"

"Not really," she said. "I believe there is something. I know there must be something. Otherwise, we wouldn't be here."

"Do you believe in fate?"

"Fate? Yeah. Definitely."

"What makes you believe in that?" I asked.

"I don't know, different kinds of things. Like meeting you."

Pausing, I continued, "Do you believe it was your fate to become a prostitute?"

"Yeah, I guess I do," she said, "That's me being punished for all the things I've done. That's the way it goes."

"Think you'll ever be able to live a normal life, and put this behind you?" I asked.

"No, never. You keep dragging it with you. If I meet a person I like, I'll have to tell him. With every relationship, you take it with you. You can't leave it behind. That wouldn't be fair. Say I just met you, and things are going great. But I never tell you, and then you find out. How would you feel? We could be walking in the city, and someone might say, 'Hey, that's the girl from the red light district!' How would you feel? If I met someone, I wouldn't tell him on the first day. But if we were together a while, and everything was going great, I would have to let him know. He could make up his mind. Are you going to stay with me, or not? Could you live with a girl who has been a prostitute? How would you feel if your friends and family found out? What would they say? They would say, 'Sorry, I'm not going to accept her.' Yes?"

I couldn't think of anything to say. I wasn't willing to concede the point. I wanted to believe it was possible. I wanted to believe I would fight for her.

"You see," she continued, interrupting the silence. "That's why I want to be honest. That's why you always drag it with you. You can't leave it behind. If I love you, and you love me, that would be the reason I would tell you. If you are in love, you tell each other everything. Just like I'm doing with you. It's a part of my life that will go on until I die. I don't think I'll ever have peace. It's something you can't forget.

"For me, it's easier to sleep with someone than start a relationship, and open my heart. For me, that's easy, real easy. Relationships are hard. When I meet someone outside work, and they know I'm a prostitute, they think, 'Hey, why not? Customers expect it, so should I.' One of the first things they say is, 'You want to come home tonight, right? Just to get laid?' So you get laid, and when you finish, you go. That's how my relationships work. If you meet a girl and you take her home, you give a part of yourself, right? I don't. I just lie there and think, another day's work, even when I'm not working. Because that's the only thing they want. I mean, life is money and sex, right? Be honest."

"I think there's more to it than that," I said.

"For young people, it's money and sex. You want to get laid? Crawl inside. You finished? Good. Thank you. Bye. Don't call me, I'll call you."

"Do you believe in love?" I asked.

"I don't know. I really don't know. I think it's more like, that's the way it goes. I wish I had it. I really do. I always think these things just don't happen to me, like meeting someone, falling in love, getting married, and having children. I don't see it."

"You want that?" I asked.

"Of course," she said quietly. "Who doesn't?"

Hearing Emma talk about how distanced she was from the world, and herself, saddened me deeply. I looked down, fighting off tears. "Where did you get those?" I asked, pointing at her dog slippers.

"They were a gift from my mom. A few weeks ago, a friend came by for a visit. She works with mentally ill people. When she saw them, she said, 'People who wear slippers like that miss love.'" Emma slid back into her slippers and curled up next to me on the couch. "But how can I miss something I've never had?" she asked.

With no answers to her questions, I continued with one of my own. "If you ever have kids, will you tell them about your time in the district?"

"No. Kids talk. Maybe my daughter would tell a friend, and the friend would tell someone else. All of a sudden, my daughter would come home saying, 'Mom, listen to what happened! I got beat up because you were a prostitute. I was called names like hooker's-child and whore-girl.'"

"How would you respond if your daughter wanted to be like you?" I asked.

"I would kill her. Then I would kill the person she wanted to work for. I made choices, but that was different. My life was already shitty, so what the hell? I would never put my kids in the same position. I got put out on the street. I blame my mother for it all. I still do. That's why our relationship will never be a good one. That's why I can't say I love her. Because of the things she's done, and the choices she's made."

"If your son wanted to visit one?" I continued.

"Why pay money? If you go to a disco, you buy a girl a cola for three guilders and screw her that night. I would be upset if he went to a prostitute. I know how prostitutes think. It's only about money. Say he works for some boss, comes home with two thousand guilders a month, and brings four hundred to a prostitute. That's a shame, isn't it? That's why I'd be mad."

"Would you take a boring desk job if you could?" I asked.

"A desk job? Absolutely! If you have a normal job, you get a fixed salary and don't have to do shit—just pick up the phone, and type a few letters. Prostitution is a job you can't work from nine to five. It's disgusting, you make long hours, and have to wait and see how many customers you get each day. As a prostitute, you think, how can I pay my bills? Oh, shit, I didn't earn diddly. I've been working my ass off, standing here smiling. It looks glamorous, and people think we make millions. I don't know why."

"There are so many beautiful women working in Amsterdam, just like you," I said. "With beauty comes power. Aren't there other ways to make a living, even now?"

Emma looked at me, paused, and said, "I think it's true what people say. The girls who get into this business have problems. Just like me. Most have no roof over their head, and are put in a situation where they can't do anything else. I mean it's nice working for a boss, but if you don't have a place to sleep at night, good luck. What do you do? Dive into a public toilet, freshen up, and go back the next day? It doesn't work that way. You can't go to a job market when you sleep on a bench. Then, once you start, it's hard to get out. The world doesn't want you back."

"What would you say to someone who thinks you're a bad person for being a prostitute?" I asked.

"People see us working and form their opinions, but they don't know how a girl feels. They don't know how she got there, or what she's had to do to survive. I think that's wrong. People should know before they say anything. People don't like us because they think we get money for lying on our backs. They should know it's not so easy. They should know you have to stand for hours and do horrible things. They should know we are still human beings. If people really knew the life of a prostitute, they wouldn't talk like that."

"Do you get nightmares?" I continued.

"Yeah, I get nightmares. I wake up and feel dirty. I sometimes go into the shower six times a day. I usually can't sleep because my day goes into night, and my night goes into day."

"How about good dreams. Do you have those too?" I asked.

"No. I'm too tired. When I sleep, I sleep." Emma let out a yawn. We had been talking for hours. It was getting late. I knew it was time to wrap things up.

"Has anything good ever come from working?" I asked, hoping to end on a positive note.

"No, nothing, except for maybe the knowledge of people. If I look at you, I can tell if you're a good person or not. I can read you without knowing you. I don't know how to explain it, but it's true."

"Have you ever befriended someone you've met in the district?"

"Only you," Emma said.

"Why me?" I asked.

"I think because of the book." She hesitated, and then laughed, "And maybe because you speak English."

"Why did you want a book?"

"I think I've always needed something to finish this chapter of my life," she said. "Now that I have it, I'm leaving, for good this time. I'm never going back. It's over."

"For real?" I asked.

"For real," she said with a sense of calm, and a tear trickling down her cheek.

I couldn't believe what I was hearing. She was getting out. By agreeing to help with the book, she had seemingly found the closure she needed, and the strength to move on. While I always believed change was possible, even for Emma, my skepticism won out. To watch her change in front of me was overwhelming, and took me by surprise. As she sat there, she seemed different. I was no longer sitting with a prostitute, but a girl who used to be one. Without being overdramatic, it was like watching a caterpillar turn into a butterfly. Looking back, the one thing she always seemed to lack was purpose. Now, with the book, she had one. But I had to be realistic and wonder how long the transformation would last.

My thoughts were brought back to the first time I saw Emma in her window, the night I gave her flowers. We had a connection from the second we met. It was undeniable. Somehow, we both knew we were meant to be in each other's lives. It just took us until now to figure out why.

The Japanese have a term for this phenomenon, rooted in legend. It's called the Red Thread of Fate, a mysterious and benevolent energy that connects two souls who are meant to change each other. Looking back, maybe this energy was what the Japanese man saw glowing around me when he sold me those roses months ago.

"This makes me happier than you will ever know," I replied, thinking the interview would end there. We had exhausted so many subjects, and it was time to call it a night. But in my heart I had one final question. I took a deep breath, and continued, "Just one more question. One more thing I need to know, and then we're done."

"Go for it," she said.

"If I had come by as a customer after we met, would you have turned me away?"

Leaning up next to me on the couch, she took my hand in hers, and said softly, "Yes. I would've turned you away. Definitely. I have a different kind of relationship with you. No, I'm sorry. You are another part of my life. You are not a customer.

"So, are we done?" she asked, a few minutes before midnight.

"We're done," I replied.

It was late, and I had a train to catch, but I didn't want to leave. Standing on the steps of her apartment, I wanted to spend the night. I had only a few hours left in Holland, and Emma was no longer a prostitute. She was now just a girl. It was now or never. However, I knew doing so would ruin everything. Our relationship was different. It wasn't about that, and never was. It had nothing to do with sex. It was about something more powerful, an intimacy on a deeper level. Amidst all the sadness, we had discovered something pure.

Emma and I walked hand in hand to the station. Every step was more difficult than the next. It felt wrong leaving her. I knew that, after tonight, I would likely never see her again.

Once at the station, we hugged, kissed on the cheeks, and said our goodbyes. "I'm finally done," she said again, tears in her eyes. "Thanks for making me matter."

"I'm going to miss you," I said, "and promise to write a book that will make you proud."

Hesitating, she said, "I'm sure you will."

My train arrived, and I was off. Whether or not I found the answers I was looking for, I felt strangely satisfied. Against all odds, a Dutch prostitute and an American had connected in the most unlikely of places, and transformed each other as a result. But I also felt empty, and a sense of loss. Just like that, she was gone.

I fell asleep and awoke as the train was pulling into the station. I smiled when I saw the Purple Rocket patiently waiting, and pedaled home. When I arrived, the usual crowd was hanging out, drinking wine. They had just made it back from a night dancing at Melkweg.

"How did it go?" Oliver asked.

"It went well," I said emotionlessly.

"What's wrong?"

"It's just sad," I said. "Regardless of what you think about prostitution, it's just sad. When I started working on this project, I was idealistic. Now, I'm left with just sadness. The district strips women of just about everything else. But in the process, I found Emma, and she's done with all that now. Her nightmare is over."

"What do you mean, she's done?" Oliver asked.

"She's leaving the district. For good."

"Are you sure? How do you know?"

"I just do," I said, handing him the keys to my bike. "Take care of her for me."

"I most certainly will," Oliver replied.

Just as I was saying my final goodbyes, I heard a familiar voice. She was walking up the stairs to the kitchen. I couldn't place it, but I knew it was someone I hadn't seen in a while.

Then I saw her. It was Inga, my Lithuanian friend who showed me the city months ago. She had left Holland during my first week. Now, she had returned to Amsterdam for one night. It so happened to be my last night in town.

I do not believe in destiny. Nor do I believe that God is always looking out over one's shoulder, or that everything happens for a reason. There could be no reason Emma spent the last five years of her life in a window. However, perhaps for the first time, I began to understand there is an order to things. Life is not completely random. There is a larger framework in which we are all a part.

I came to Amsterdam wanting to write a book. Little did I know, from the moment I arrived, I had a job to do. It had now been accomplished, and it was time to say goodbye. I wasn't ready to leave, but my time was up. Then, there was Inga. She was there for me on my first night. Now, she magically appeared on my last. She had taken me in, and was sending me off. It was hard to explain.

Inga smiled when she saw me. I smiled back.

"Amsterdam is in my heart," I said to her, as my last day in Holland came to an end.

Chapter 26

THE NEXT DAY I flew home to America. In the ensuing year, I would graduate from law school, take the New York bar exam, travel to Morocco, and start my life as a litigator. Amsterdam seemed like a dream, but I still thought about Emma. I relived our time together in my mind, and regretted not letting her know the depth of my feelings. Much was left unsaid.

Mostly, though, I worried she had returned to the district. It's hard breaking habits. I knew it wouldn't be easy. Communicating was tough, but we occasionally emailed. All she ever wanted to know about was the book, and when it would be finished. She shared few details about her life. All I could tell her was that I was working on it. After a while, she stopped asking. Her guard, once down, had been raised. I remained committed to the book, but needed time and perspective, two things I didn't have.

When Thanksgiving rolled around, I flew to Amsterdam on a red-eye to reunite with my graduate school friends. Meeting in Amsterdam for the holiday had become a bit of a tradition. Really, though, the trip was an excuse to see Emma. A year had passed. I had no idea what to expect. When I let her know I was visiting, she insisted on picking me up at the airport. She would have it no other way. But she warned she had a surprise, so I should be ready.

After a sleepless night, I arrived at Schiphol Airport with 50 guilders in my pocket. I had kept them as a reminder of my time in Amsterdam. They grounded me, and assured me my time there was real. From the moment I stepped off the plane, they gave me the feeling I was returning home. In many ways, I had never left.

Once I made it through customs, I looked for Emma. I knew there was a chance she might not show. She had disappeared on me so many times before. After scanning the crowd, she was nowhere to be found. But then I saw her, and I saw her surprise. She was standing with a man, and holding a baby in her arms.

While much had changed in my life, more had changed in hers. We grabbed coffee in the airport and she filled me in. As promised, she hadn't returned to the district, but took a job in Utrecht helping troubled kids get their lives back on track. It was the same job she had before she started work in Arnhem years ago. The guy was her fiancé and father of her two-month-old girl. When I asked when they were getting married, Emma scoffed and said she hadn't set a date. She was in no rush, and wasn't even wearing a ring. Her fiancé sat there, staring at me. I could only wonder what he'd heard. I was uncertain about the guy, and something felt wrong. Emma could do better.

After finishing my coffee and complimentary cookie, we loaded into her car. Sitting in the back with her baby, Emma drove the four of us to her new apartment in Utrecht. It was a surreal experience to say the least, and made even more surreal by my state of exhaustion. Jet lag hit me hard, and it felt like I was stepping back into a dream, but not the same dream as before. Time had passed. Things were different.

Sitting in the back of her car, I had no idea where the day might lead. I started getting nervous. I had no book to deliver. Maybe Emma felt betrayed. Maybe she thought I was full of shit. Maybe her new guy was there to do something about it. My only reassurance came from the look in her eyes when she greeted me at the airport. It was the same look from when she said goodbye a year ago. Much had changed, but our feelings remained.

Thanksgiving was scheduled for six in the evening, which gave me five hours to reconnect with my old friend. Hopefully we would have some time alone. With her fiancé lurking and suspicious, it wasn't going to be easy.

After stopping for gas and Red Bull, we arrived at Emma's home. She had recently left her apartment in Houten for a less expensive flat in a high-rise. After leaving the district and having a baby, she needed to downsize. She said she hated the place, and felt boxed in. During the visit, all Emma wanted to know about was the book, which was far from finished.

"Books like this take time," I said. "It'll get done. I promise."

She wasn't happy, but dropped the subject and went into the kitchen to make grilled cheese sandwiches. When I tried following her, she stopped me. "No one is allowed in my kitchen but me," she said. "You know the rules." With nowhere to go, I sat on the couch with her fiancé. The guy didn't speak much English, and watched me like a hawk. Never once did he show Emma any affection. After a few uncomfortable hours of meaningless chitchat and watching television, Emma said it was time to leave.

"Where're we going?" I asked.

"My mom's house. She wants to meet you."

Given my feelings for Emma, it was difficult spending time with her fiancé. Now, her mom was being thrown into the mix. After hearing Emma's stories, I wasn't a fan. I had no idea why it was so important for me to meet her. I figured Emma had her reasons.

Emma drove the four of us to her mom's house a few kilometers away. She lived in a small, two-story condo in a middle-class neighborhood. She greeted us at the door without saying a word. She just looked me up and down, and lit a cigarette.

I eventually broke the silence. "I've heard a lot about you," I said.

"Likewise," she said, gesturing for me to come inside and offering a coffee.

We sat on a couch and turned on the TV. Her mom just sat there, chain-smoking. She took so little interest in me I wondered why we'd come. It had now been over four hours, and my reunion with Emma was less than spectacular.

With minutes to go before I had to leave, Emma said, "David, I need to show you something upstairs. It came this week. It's my wedding dress." Looking at her fiancé, she said, "You can't come. You know, bad luck." I walked behind Emma into her mom's bedroom. She closed the door. For the first time that day, we were alone.

Her wedding dress was folded in a box beneath the bed. Without saying a word, Emma took it out, and held it in front of her.

"You look beautiful," I said.

"You really think so?" she asked.

"Of course," I replied.

"You need to know something. I've never fallen for a customer. Then you came along, refusing to be one." She paused, and continued, "That's why I haven't set a date for the wedding. Just ask me, say the words, and I'm yours."

In that moment, as Emma stood there, trembling, so many thoughts raced through my mind. I remembered the first time I saw her. I remembered how beautiful she looked that night, and every day that followed. I remembered how much we taught each other, and the trust we built. I remembered my trip to the Mustang Ranch, and the first time I thought about writing a book about prostitution. I remembered how little I once knew, and reflected on how much I had come to understand. Finally, I remembered the conversation I had with my friend at Oxford, when he spoke about Einstein and explained that every moment in life is happening, over and over, in perpetuity. I found comfort in his words, but not enough. I didn't just want the moments we shared to repeat. I wanted new ones as well.

Looking at Emma, as she held up her wedding dress, tears flooding her eyes, I wanted nothing more than to make her smile and rush into my arms. I wanted so badly to say the words, and for us to sail off into the sunset. They just weren't there. I couldn't disrupt her life and all she had created. She was a mom now, and engaged. Our time together had run its course. Deep down, despite the sincerity of her words, I think she knew that, too. But it didn't make things any easier.

With the sun setting and her family waiting downstairs, all I could do was give her a hug. She hugged me back, both of us knowing we had already gone much further than either of us could have ever imagined.

Epilogue

AS OF THE publication of this book, that was the last time I had any contact with Emma. Today, I can only hope she is happily married, and as promised, never returned to the district. While working on this book, it was never my intention to pass judgment on the world of prostitution, in Amsterdam or elsewhere. Rather, it was my intention to cast new light on the red light district and the women who work there. But just like when rafting down a river, the journey that unfolded was largely out of my control, as were the lessons learned and conclusions reached.

At some point, every girl dreams of what she wants to be when she grows up. Some dream of becoming a lawyer, a doctor, or a teacher. No child ever dreams of becoming a whore. So what happens? Why do thousands of women each year choose to become prostitutes in Holland, America, and elsewhere? While Emma entered the profession because she needed a roof over her head, and money, there was something more.

Just as the cab driver explained on the way to the Mustang Ranch, I believe people generally end up in life where they think they belong, and make their own choices, whether they are able to come to terms with that or not. However, the choices that appear available are subjective. Perspective can be warped.

Emma ended up in the district because she believed she belonged there. No one told her any different. Not even her family. In her mind, the forces of her life directed her there. After being abandoned, abused, and ultimately put out on the streets, the district became her calling, her place in the world. The same holds true for countless others. As Shannon L. Alder writes, "Your life perspective comes from the cage you are held captive in."

Writing this book was filled with sadness. The sadness of realizing there is little society can do to keep a woman from working as a prostitute. If that's where she feels she belongs, that's where she'll go. Nothing can change that. Once the decision is made, there's no turning back. Once a whore, always a whore, or so these women are led to believe. They try it because they wrongfully think they belong there, only later to be told by society there they must stay. They are criminals. They are subhuman. They no longer count.

I do not expect anyone to have much empathy for Emma after reading this book, or for any of the other women mentioned. Despite Emma's upbringing, no one forced her to become a prostitute. Sure, she had a tough life and some bad luck, but she made her own choices. Nor do I expect anyone to approve of her profession. I only ask that you remember that Emma, and others like her, are people. They are alive. They count. They have souls, and still have important choices to make. We as a society should help them make the right ones, rather than condemn them to relive their mistakes over and over again.

So, the next time, for whatever reason, you are about to call someone a whore, hooker, harlot, tramp, strumpet, fallen woman, or any other colorful alternative, I ask that you think of Emma and this story. Give yourself pause. Words can have consequences. They can keep people in their cells, and can hurt. We should be more careful. I know Emma would appreciate it, and countless others would too.

Deep down, this book is not about Emma, or prostitution, or even Amsterdam. Rather, it's about humanity. It's about how society tries to impose its will on all of us, and the enduring nature of the human spirit. It's about believing that change is possible. It's about being willing to color outside the lines, even if that means entering forbidden territory, as doing so can make a difference, and perhaps change a life. Most of all, it's about the inherent worth of the individual.

The moment I bought Emma those roses could not be planned, imagined, or duplicated. Our relationship was genuine, and forced me to rethink my understanding of so many things. I learned about love, the many forms of it, and how society creates limitations on whom we can love, and whom we can't. Emma and I shared something powerful. We stepped outside the box. We let ourselves enter into a relationship unlike any before. It wasn't about sex. It wasn't about control, nor was it about security or safety. It was about connectivity, and was liberating for both of us.

The love we had was platonic. It had to be. That's what made it so perfect.

Almost every day, I would pass a huge digital clock on Haarlemmerstraat. It counted down the seconds to the millennium. Many thought Y2K would bring about the end of time. It didn't, but the looming possibility magnified every second of my life in Holland. I was not living on autopilot. I was immersed in every moment as if it might be my last. I was dreaming while awake, and had control of my story. So many of us live our lives worrying about the past and anxious about the future, never once stepping foot in the present. When we live this way, life passes us by. During my time in Holland, I hadn't only stepped foot in the present. I was stomping on it.

One of the great joys of living abroad is being off the grid, and being free from the hierarchical nature of society. In America and elsewhere, so many of us compare our situation to those around us, taking pride in being above others in the hierarchy. The problem is, while there may be people beneath you, there will always be people above, leading to a never-ending struggle to be someone else, a constant state of dissatisfaction. In many ways, this is the root of so much pain and evil in our world. By shifting to a horizontal way of thinking, things change. The world becomes less threatening, and more accessible. I never thought of myself as being above Emma, or any of the other women in the district, just differently situated. I think this is one of the things Emma saw in my eyes when we met. It was one of the things that allowed us to connect.

There was something else too. When I set out to write this book, there were two things I told myself I could never do: pay a prostitute to talk, or sleep with one. I had a code, and followed it. Not only did it provide me with purpose, it provided a framework upon which Emma could hold on to. It made all the difference in our story, and her ability to move on.

In my wildest dreams, I never imagined working on this book would lead to Emma quitting the profession. Few things have made me happier. By chance, if any working girls happen to stumble on this book, I hope the story inspires you to make similar choices. With Emma, it all started with her developing a speck of self-worth. Once she realized she mattered, everything followed from there. The book simply helped her realize what was true all along.

Ultimately, I wrote this book because I felt it was a journey so worth going on I needed to share it with others. So thanks for traveling down this road with me, or shall I say, floating down this river. True, questions were left unanswered. Particularly, who was that mystery man? Did Emma get married, and most importantly, did she ever return to the district? Everything did not become clear in the end. It rarely does. Essentially, this book was about my struggle to write about the district, and everything that happened along the way. Appropriate, because in life, it's always about the journey. Then the journey ends. Sometimes endings are epic, but usually not.

The last time I saw Emma, she asked me to marry her. I just stood there speechless. The moment she held up her wedding dress, I loved her more than ever, but I knew our story had run its course. For us, there would be no Hollywood ending. But our love was real, and we both knew it.

Without a doubt, I still think about her. It makes me happy knowing I meant something to her. I never became a customer, and finally had what I needed for my book. After all, that was the goal from the start. My journey through the red light district was complete. Mission accomplished. We defied the odds and did the impossible. That should have been enough. But, alas, just like in life, you are always left wanting more.

Letter to Emma

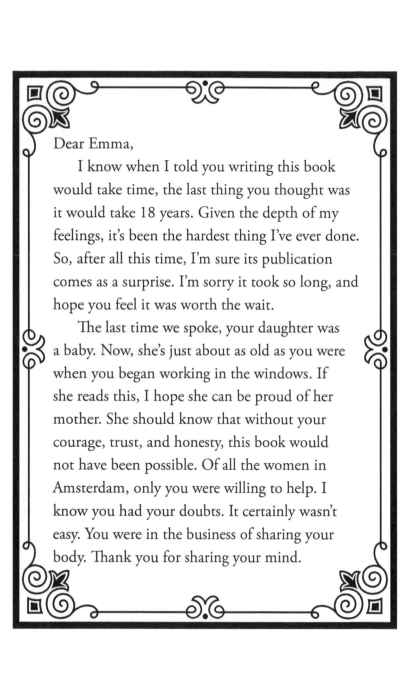

Dear Emma,

I know when I told you writing this book would take time, the last thing you thought was it would take 18 years. Given the depth of my feelings, it's been the hardest thing I've ever done. So, after all this time, I'm sure its publication comes as a surprise. I'm sorry it took so long, and hope you feel it was worth the wait.

The last time we spoke, your daughter was a baby. Now, she's just about as old as you were when you began working in the windows. If she reads this, I hope she can be proud of her mother. She should know that without your courage, trust, and honesty, this book would not have been possible. Of all the women in Amsterdam, only you were willing to help. I know you had your doubts. It certainly wasn't easy. You were in the business of sharing your body. Thank you for sharing your mind.

When I started, I had no idea how this book would unfold. I had no idea I would be writing about a special friendship I would develop with a special girl. I had no idea it would be so personal. But that is what happened. You have touched me deeply. You have changed the way I see the world. Now, you will change the way others see the world too. Something good will come from all those years in the windows after all.

As requested, you will remain anonymous to anyone reading this book—of course, unless you choose otherwise. I'll leave that up to you. But I know who you are, and remember our time together like it was yesterday. As I write my final thoughts, I can only think that maybe our paths will cross once again. I wouldn't be surprised. Somehow, we are connected.

About the Author

David Wienir is a business affairs executive at United Talent Agency and entertainment law instructor at UCLA Extension. Before UTA, he practiced law at two of the top entertainment law firms where he represented clients such as Steven Spielberg and Madonna. This is his fourth book. Previous books include *Last Time: Labour's Lessons from the Sixties* (co-authored with a Member of Parliament at the age of 23), *The Diversity Hoax: Law Students Report from Berkeley* (afterword by Dennis Prager), and *Making It on Broadway: Actors' Tales of Climbing to the Top* (foreword by Jason Alexander).

Before becoming a lawyer, he was a professional river rafting guide, a speechwriter in the British House of Commons, and a host of *Estonia Today* on Estonia National Radio. He is also a founder and the first musical director of the *Oxford Alternotives*, Oxford University's oldest a cappella close harmony group. He was educated at Columbia, Oxford, The LSE, Berkeley Law, and the Vrije Universiteit Amsterdam, and is married to Dr. Dina, a pioneer of the medical cannabis movement and the inspiration for the Nancy Botwin character in the show *Weeds*. They live in West Hollywood with their teacup Brazilian Yorkie named Lola.

Thanks for reading Amsterdam Exposed and please consider sharing your thoughts on Amazon and on other platforms.

DISCARD

CPSIA information can be obtained
at www.ICGtesting.com
Printed in the USA
LVHW04s1615200418
574264LV00001B/123/P